# IF YOU LOVE THIS BOOK,
please take a moment to post a review or tell a friend.

## DO YOU HAVE A BOOK IDEA?
We're looking for authors who can inspire with expert knowledge. Submit your proposal:

www.schifferbooks.com/submitabookproposal

Pop Culture | Art & Design | Fine Craft & Technique
Fashion & Fiber Arts | Architecture & Interior Design
Decorative Arts | Regional

Divination | Meditation | Astrology | Psychic Skills
Numerology & Palmistry | Channeled Material
Metaphysics | Spirituality | Health & Lifestyle

Aerospace | Naval | Ground Forces
American Civil War | Militaria | Uniforms & Insignia
Weaponry | Modeling | Transportation

Early Concepts | SEED | STEAM
Laptime & Independent Reading | Interactive Learning
Board Books | Picture Books | Middle Grade

---

**SCHIFFER PUBLISHING, LTD.**
4880 Lower Valley Road | Atglen, PA 19310
610-593-1777 | info@schifferbooks.com

**www.schifferbooks.com**

Printed in India

# COLLECTIBLE CAST IRON

## Bundt Pans and Gugelhupf Cake Forms

**JOHN BRIGGS**
The Cast Iron Chef

4880 Lower Valley Road · Atglen, PA 19310

Copyright © 2025 by John Briggs

Library of Congress Control Number: 2024942482

All rights reserved. No part of this work may be reproduced or used in any form or by any means—graphic, electronic, or mechanical, including photocopying or information storage and retrieval systems—without written permission from the publisher.

The scanning, uploading, and distribution of this book or any part thereof via the Internet or any other means without the permission of the publisher is illegal and punishable by law. Please purchase only authorized editions and do not participate in or encourage the electronic piracy of copyrighted materials.

"Schiffer," "Schiffer Publishing, Ltd.," and the pen and inkwell logo are registered trademarks of Schiffer Publishing, Ltd.

Edited by Ian Robertson
Designed by Beth Oberholtzer
Cover design by Alexa Harris
Type set in Gin/Trebuchet/Avenir Next/Minion Pro/Web Symbols

ISBN: 978-0-7643-6935-3
Printed in India

Published by Schiffer Publishing, Ltd.
4880 Lower Valley Road
Atglen, PA 19310
Phone: (610) 593-1777; Fax: (610) 593-2002
Email: info@schifferbooks.com
Web: www.schifferbooks.com

For our complete selection of fine books on this and related subjects, please visit our website at www.schifferbooks.com. You may also write for a free catalog.

Schiffer Publishing's titles are available at special discounts for bulk purchases for sales promotions or premiums. Special editions, including personalized covers, corporate imprints, and excerpts, can be created in large quantities for special needs. For more information, contact the publisher.

## TRADEMARKS

All-Clad®
Berkley Machine Works & Foundry Co.
Bundt™
Buzuluk a.s.
Le Creuset / Cousances
Eisenwerk Lauchhammer
Eisenwerk Martinlamitz GmbH
Frank'sche Eisenwerk GmbH
Gottbill sel Erben Eisenwerk GmbH
Griswold Manufacturing Co.
Frank W Hay & Sons
J. C. Roberts
John Wright Company
Lodge Manufacturing Company, the Lodge "Legacy" Series
Pillsbury
Pillsbury Bake-Off
Northland Aluminum Products, Inc.
Nordic Ware, Inc.
Savery & Company Iron Hollow Ware Foundry
Wagner Manufacturing Company
Węgierska Górka Eisenwerk
Železárny a Smaltovny Bartelmus a.s.
*Ein new Kochbuch* by Marx Rupolt's (Wikipedia Commons)
Nordic Ware Bundt™ Pan, Smithsonian Museum of American History (Public Domain)
Ella Helfrich and her prize-winning Tunnel of Fudge Bundt cake, 1966. Copyright General Mills, Inc.

*I would like to thank my family for all the support it took for me to write this collector's guide, especially my wife, Katie. We are the lucky ones. Also our "fab five" daughters: Molly, Paloma, Eimile, Hannah, and Christina, who have been the lucky beneficiaries of the cakes baked in all these wonderful pans.*

# Contents

| | |
|---|---|
| **Preface** | 7 |
| **Acknowledgments** | 9 |
| **Terminology** | 10 |
| **History** | 11 |
| Europe—Gugelhupf Cake Forms | 11 |
| The United States—the American Bundt® Pan | 12 |
| **Collectible Market** | 14 |
| Buying Tips | 14 |
| Marked Pans | 15 |
| Foundry Marks | 16 |
| Foundry Numbers and Letters | 16 |
| Custom Foundry Marks | 17 |
| Owner's Marks | 18 |
| **Dating Unmarked Pans** | 19 |
| Sprue Marks and Gate Marks | 19 |
| Handles | 20 |
| Enameled Pans | 22 |
| **Pan Styles** | 23 |
| Traditional Style | 23 |
| Crown Style | 23 |
| Fluted Style | 24 |
| Swirl Style | 24 |
| **Named Pans** | 25 |
| "Triple Crown" Series | 25 |
| **Known Collectible Bundt and Gugelhupf Pans** | 27 |
| Berkley Machine Works & Foundry Company (Norfolk, Virginia) | 28 |
| Cousances–Le Creuset (Cousances-les-Forges, France) | 39 |
| Eisenwerk Lauchhammer (Lauchhammer-Ost, Germany) | 41 |
| Eisenwerk Lauchhammer | 42 |
| Eisenwerk Martinlamitz GmbH (Schwarzenbach an der Saale, Germany) | 45 |
| Eisenwerk Martinlamitz GmbH | 46 |
| Frank'sche Eisenwerk GmbH, Adolfshütte (Hesse, Germany) | 47 |
| Gottbill sel Erben Eisenwerk (Mariahütte, Germany) | 51 |
| Griswold Manufacturing Company | 64 |
| Frank W Hay & Sons (Griswold) | 66 |
| J. C. Roberts | 67 |
| John Wright Company | 68 |
| Lodge Manufacturing Company | 69 |
| Savery and Company Iron Hollow Ware Foundry | 72 |
| Wagner Manufacturing Company | 73 |
| Węgierska Górka Eisenwerk (Węgierska Górka, Poland) | 78 |
| Železárny a Smaltovny Bartelmus a.s. (Pilsen, Czech Republic) | 80 |
| **Unknown Traditional-Style Bundt and Gugelhupf Pans** | 83 |
| **Unknown Crown-Style Bundt and Gugelhupf Pans** | 99 |
| **Unknown Fluted-Style Bundt and Gugelhupf Pans** | 113 |
| **Unknown Swirl-Style Bundt and Gugelhupf Pans** | 123 |
| **Unknown Bundt and Gugelhupf Cake Forms** | 141 |
| **Recasts of Nordic Ware Pans** | 145 |
| **"Baby Bundts"** | 148 |
| **Appendix: Research Data** | 149 |
| Known European Foundry Marks | 150 |
| Unknown Foundry Marks | 152 |
| Berkley Machine Works & Foundry Company—the "Pilgrim" | 153 |
| Buzuluk a.s, Muzeum Komárov | 155 |
| Traditional-Style Gugelhupf Pan Marked "C&H" | 156 |
| Gottbill ser Erben Logos and Marks | 157 |

| | |
|---|---|
| Gottbill ser Erben 1933 Product Catalog | 158 |
| Eisenwerk Lauchhammer, Foundry Logos and Foundry Marks | 159 |
| Eisenwerk Lauchhammer, Kunstgussmuseum Lauchhammer | 160 |
| Frank'sche Eisenwerk GmbH, Adolfshütte | 161 |
| The "Reichsritter" Swirl-Style Gugelhupf Pan, Marked "ERM" | 162 |
| History of Węgierska Górka Eisenwerk Foundry Marks | 163 |

| | |
|---|---|
| **Glossary** | 165 |
| **Bibliography** | 167 |
| **Notes** | 169 |
| **Index** | 171 |
| **About the Author** | 173 |

# Preface

I grew up eating my mother's "Bundt" cakes. I also remember the unusual-looking cake pan with the funny tube in the middle of it. Little did I know that fifty years later I would become an avid collector of these pans and eventually author a collector's guide.

For several years I have been collecting American cast iron, primarily Erie, Griswold, and Wapak Indian Head pans. I had gone to culinary school at Le Cordon Bleu in San Francisco and had been a sous chef at La Petite Rive in Mendocino, California. Later I launched a food blog called *The Cast Iron Chef*, in which I posted many of my favorite recipes that I had adapted to cooking with my vintage cast-iron pans.

Eventually, after publishing more than one hundred culinary recipes for cast iron, I turned to baking. Baking opened opportunities to explore everything from biscuits to coffee cake and scones for breakfast, as well as recipes such as dinner rolls, focaccia, and cornbread for sides with lunch and dinner. That left dessert. I had already acquired a Griswold loaf pan and a set of Waterman gem pans, which enabled me to post recipes for various loaf breads and gem pan recipes. What remained for me was cakes.

This led me to acquire my first cast-iron Bundt pan. It was a smaller pan, shaped somewhat like a crown, with an unfamiliar mark on it and the number "22." My first attempt to bake a cake with this pan was a disaster. I tried to make the infamous "Tunnel of Fudge" cake, which is easily the most famous Bundt cake recipe in the US. When the cake came out of the oven, it crumbled to pieces when I tried to remove it from the pan. I quickly realized that, like many of my other culinary recipes, baking recipes would also have to be adapted for cast iron. I quickly found the solution by researching cast-iron cooking groups online.

I was also curious as to the foundry marks on my Bundt pan. All my other cast-iron pans had clear marks from foundries such as "Erie," "Griswold," "Lodge," and "Wagner," but the mark on my Bundt pan was a mystery to me. I quickly found out that my pan was part of one of the biggest mysteries among cast-iron collectors, especially those of cast-iron Bundt pans. All that was known about my pan was that it was of German origin, known as a "gugelhupf" pan, and that the "22" represented the diameter of the pan in centimeters.

It turns out that my pan was one of ten different examples with the same mark. These ten gugelhupf pans represented some of the most popular Bundt pans in the collector community, but no one knew what foundry had cast the pans. This is not an uncommon problem with cast-iron pans from Germany. Many of the cast-iron foundries in Germany were converted to support the German military during WWI and WWII. Unfortunately for these foundries, this made them prime military targets. The result was that many of the foundries were destroyed, along with all their records, catalogs, patterns, and molds. Little information was left behind for collectors to research and catalog the foundry marks on many of the most collectible pans cast in Germany.

Fortunately for me, just about the time I acquired my mystery German Bundt pan, an important discovery was made. An unused cast-iron roaster, with the same foundry mark as on my Bundt pan, was located with the original paper logo still attached. This identified all pans with this mark as made by the Carl Gottbill sel Erben foundry in Mariahütte, Germany.

Many European cast-iron Bundt pans have other unknown foundry marks on them. There is a small, dedicated group of enthusiasts who are actively involved in the search to discover the foundries associated with these pans. As a newly retired tech executive with idle hands, I enthusiastically joined in the search. As part of my research, I began acquiring European gugelhupf pans that evolved into more of a research archive than a collection.

After years of research, and with more than 120 gugelhupf pans now in my "archive," I have been able to identify three additional foundries accounting for fourteen previously unidentified gugelhupf pans. More than fifty popular gugelhupf pans remain unidentified, so the search continues. This collector's guide contains everything I have learned to date. I hope to make regular updates as new discoveries are made in the coming years.

# Acknowledgments

This collector's guide has truly been a five-year group effort, with input provided from many of the leading dealers and collectors of cast-iron Bundt pans. Without their assistance this guide could not have been written. Not only have they provided much of the key information in this guide, but I am also happy to say that many of them have become my friends along the way.

First and foremost I would like to thank EJ Bogusch. EJ was instrumental not only in establishing the collector community of cast-iron Bundt pans, but also in inventing the naming convention that was so desperately needed to identify each unknown collectible Bundt pan. This was necessary because many if not most of the collectible cast-iron Bundt pans are unmarked and come from unknown foundries. EJ also provided some of the images used in this guide, made a major contribution to the "Buying Tips" section, and fact-checked the US collector market for me.

I would also like to thank Marc Wissen, my "feet on the ground" in Germany. Not only is Marc the premier dealer of gugelhupf pans in Germany, but he also helps me research, translate, and procure rare cast-iron gugelhupf pans that can be purchased only locally in Europe. Without Marc, I would not have the archive I have, which has formed the backbone of this collector's guide. I would also like to thank the other members of "Team Germany" for their many contributions to this guide, including Marc Struemper, Holger Bogun, Gunther Karl Kunsthendal, and Jens Duha.

A good collector's guide is only as good as its pricing information. Much appreciated is the current pricing information provided by Chris Kendall. Between his in-person sales at flea markets and online sales with the Patriot Cast Iron and Cutlery group on Facebook, Chris probably handles more cast iron sales transactions than anyone in the country.

A good collector's guide is only as good as its pricing information. Much appreciated is the latest pricing information provided by Chris Kendall. Between his in-person sales at flea markets and online sales with the Patriot Cast Iron and Cutlery group on Facebook, Chris probably handles more cast iron sales transactions than anyone in the country.

Many thanks go out to Rhonda "the Bundt Gal" Owen for her contributions, which include sharing images from her collection and fact-checking and proofreading my manuscript. I think between the two of us we have just about every known cast-iron Bundt pan in our respective collections.

I would also like to thank Laurie Smith Monsees, who was my unofficial editor prior to having my manuscript picked up by Schiffer Publishing. Also Betsy Loveless and Elizabeth Povlich Devaney for reviewing, fact-checking, and editing the manuscript. I am not a writer by trade and could not have written this book without all their insight and support.

Lastly, I'd like to thank members of my family who spent many hours helping me catalog, measure, weigh, and photograph most of the Bundt pans in this guide. I know they do not understand my cast-iron Bundt pan obsession, but I appreciate all the encouragement and support they provided me regardless.

# Terminology

A quick note about the terminology used in this guide. A "Bundt" pan is an Americanized version of the European "gugelhupf" cake pan. In southern Germany they were also referred to as *Bundkuchen* (group cake) pans and were served at large gatherings.[1] In the Alsace region of eastern France, where gugelhupf pastries are extremely popular, the pans are known as *kouglof, kougelhof,* or *kougelhopf* pans. In the Czech Republic they are known as *babovka* (grandmother) pans. German gugelhupf pans are by far the most prevalent and popular European Bundt pans among the collector community in the United States.

Northland Aluminum Products, Inc. (later renamed "Nordic Ware, Inc."), an American company, trademarked the word "Bundt" for their version of "bundkuchen pan." So technically (and legally), when someone refers to a "Bundt" pan, they are referring to what is usually an aluminum bundkuchen-style cake pan manufactured by Northland.

In the 1960s, Northland's Bundt® pans became so popular in the US that the word "Bundt" became synonymous to most Americans for all Bundt-style, fluted cake pans of this design, regardless of whether they were manufactured by Northland, what material the pan was made of, or whether it came from the US or Europe. This is why the popular Lodge "Bundt" cast-iron pan is called the "traditional-style fluted cake pan." If they had called it a "Bundt" pan, they would be violating Northland's trademark.

Because of the Northland trademark, I will use "Bundt®" to refer to Northland's pans and will use "Bundt" or "gugelhupf" when referring to all other non-Northland "Bundt" cast-iron fluted cake pans.

# History

## Europe–Gugelhupf Cake Forms

A gugelhupf cake is a yeast-based cake, traditionally baked in a "gugelhupf" cake pan. The unique hole in the center allows cakes to bake evenly, and the ornate "forms" of the pans allow for elegant and elaborate designs, compared to the flat cakes most baked in the US.

Gugelhupf cakes are popular in a wide region of central Europe, particularly in the Alsace region of France, Germany, and the Czech Republic. They are also popular in Austria, Switzerland, Croatia, Hungary, Bosnia, Serbia, Slovakia, Slovenia, and Poland. They are also closely related to the Christmas cake in Italy, known as the *panettone*. Depending on the region, a traditional gugelhupf can contain dried fruit, almonds, chocolate chips, or even "Kirschwasser" cherry brandy. Some regional varieties (Hungarian, Czech, and Slovakian) are filled with a layer of sweetened ground poppy seeds.[2]

According to the *Grimm German dictionary*, the term "gugelhupf" is most likely derived from two different German words. The first word being "gugelhut," which is the term for a "hooded hat". The second is the word "hüpfen," which refers to a cake that rises as a result of yeast.

The earliest known gugelhupf recipe was found in Marx Rupolt's 1581 cookbook *Ein new Kochbuch* ("A new cookbook"), which contained more than two thousand recipes and was the first textbook for professional chefs in training. The recipe describes a "Hat Cake" resembling the shape of a medieval hat.[3]

The gugelhupf was also popular in the Austro-Hungarian Empire, eventually becoming standardized in Viennese cookbooks as a refined, rich cake flavored with rosewater and almonds. The cake was popularized both by Emperor Franz Joseph of Austria and earlier by his aunt Marie-Antoinette in France. So, when she reportedly said, "Let them eat cake" upon being told that the peasants had no bread, she may have been referring to gugelhupfs!

Depending on the region, antique gugelhupf cake pans were made of ceramics, cast iron, tin, and copper. For centuries, copper was common in many cooking utensils in aristocratic kitchens. It had the advantage of being easy to manufacture and conducted heat well. The disadvantage was the bright-bluish-green patina that eventually formed on the pans was toxic. Because of this, the pans had to be tinned on the interior cooking surface and constantly checked for defects in the tin.

Many collectible cast-iron gugelhupf pans originate in Germany. But many territories of what we now call "France" were also once considered parts of Germany, particularly the Alsace region. Because of this, many collectible gugelhupf pans we believe to be German were cast in what we now consider parts of France.

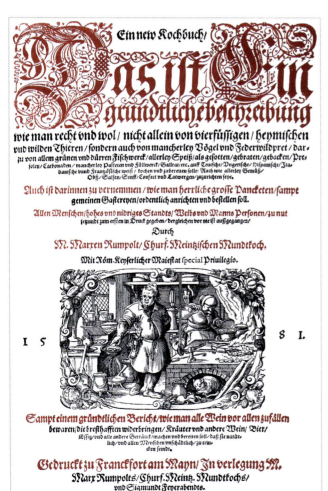

*Marx Rupolt's 1581 cookbook Ein new Kochbuch*

Northland Bundt Pattern at the the Smithsonian Museum[4]

*Courtesy of the General Mills Archives*

## The United States— the American Bundt® Pan

In 1950, three German immigrants—Rose Joshua, Fannie Shanfield, and Mary Abrahamson—from the women's Zionist group Hadassah approached David Dalquist, then president of Minneapolis-based Northland Aluminum Products, Inc. They asked if Northland could create for them the German gugelhupf pans (or "bundkuchen" pans as they were called in southern Germany) that they remembered their mothers using when they were kids.

Unfortunately, because many of the German gugelhupf pans were made of cast iron and were very heavy (some weighing more than 15 pounds!), most of them had to be left behind in Germany when the families immigrated to the US.

Mary Abrahamson's family was one of the few families that had brought their family "bundkuchen" pan to the United States, so they were able to provide Dalquist with an actual pan from which he could make a pattern.[5]

Northland Aluminum Products, Inc., had only recently been founded in 1946 by Dotty and Dave Dalquist. Dave, who was newly back from WWII,[6] saw this as an opportunity to expand their business, so he gave it a try. Dalquist and company engineer Don Nygren designed a cast aluminum mold based on Mary Abrahamson's original bundkuchen pan.

In 1950, Northland made a small production run of their newly designed pan. Dalquist shortened the name down from "bundkuchen" to "bund" and added the "t" at the end of the word so that Americans would pronounce "bund" the German way. It also enabled Northland to trademark their new pan the "Bundt®" pan.

For the first few years, sales of the Northland "Bundt®" pan were relatively low. At one point, Northland even considered discontinuing it.[7] Then, in 1966 a woman by the name of Ella Helfrich famously entered her "Tunnel of Fudge" recipe in the annual Pillsbury Bake-Off, which was wildly popular at the time. Using a Northland Bundt® pan, she came up with a recipe for a chocolate nut Bundt cake that mysteriously develops a "tunnel of fudge" filling as it bakes.[8] Ella achieved this by ingeniously including powdered frosting in the recipe. The original recipe called for Pillsbury's "Double Dutch Dry Frosting Mix," which would, in the oven, cook into a runny, pudding-like "tunnel."[9]

Ella did not win the competition; she came in second and won $5,000. Despite not winning, her recipe became so popular that Northland received more than 200,000 requests for Bundt® pans within days of the competition.

Following the huge success of the Pillsbury Bake-Off, Dotty Dalquist spent hours in the kitchen developing recipes for the Northland Bundt® pan. In October 1969, David pitched the idea for a line of boxed Bundt® cake mixes to Pillsbury's executives. Dotty baked the cakes for the pitch, which took place on their boat on Lake Superior. The idea was well received. Pillsbury ended up licensing the name "Bundt" from Northland and, for the next fifteen years, sold a line of specialized Bundt® pan cake mixes.

In 1972, Pillsbury and Northland (now "Nordic Ware, Inc.") also collaborated on a wildly successful promotion where consumers could purchase a box of Pillsbury Bundt cake mix and a Nordic Ware Bundt pan together at supermarkets for just $1.98,[10] further ensuring that the Nordic Ware Bundt pan would become a staple in every American kitchen.

Nordic Ware is now the world's leading provider of Bundt-style fluted cake pans. Nordic Ware Bundt pans can now be found in more than seventy-five million households around the world.[11]

The original Bundt pan created by Northland became so iconic that the original pattern made by Northland now sits in the Smithsonian National Museum of American History.[12]

As the popularity of the American Bundt-style pan grew, other companies, including Griswold, Wagner, and Lodge, entered the market with similar traditional Bundt-style designs. A major difference was that their pans were made of cast iron, much like many of the traditional gugelhupf pans from Europe.

Ultimately, American cast-iron foundries could not compete with Northland's line of aluminum Bundt pans. Customers preferred the aluminum pans because they were a lot lighter than cast-iron pans. They were also a lot cheaper than cast-iron pans because Nordic Ware pans could be inexpensively mass produced, and their lighter weight made shipping costs less expensive. In addition, the cooking surface on aluminum pans is much smoother compared to cooking surfaces on a cast-iron pan, making them easier to bake with compared to the more porous Bundt pans made of cast iron.

Ultimately, the lack of demand for cast-iron Bundt pans in the US made them somewhat rare, and therefore desirable for collectors of cast-iron cookware. Unlike in most European foundries, most collectible American Bundt-style pans date from 1950 onward and are, with a few exceptions, well marked and well documented.

# Collectible Market

The most-popular cast-iron Bundt pans cast in the US came from well-known foundries, including Griswold, Wagner, and Lodge. Besides the "big three," there are also some highly collectible Bundt pans available from some lesser-known US foundries, including J. C. Reynolds, John Wright Company, and Savery & Co. In addition, there are quite a few nice unmarked Bundt pans floating around from unknown US foundries.

With a few exceptions (most notably the John Wright "Fruit Top" pan, the "Washington Cake Pan" from Savery, and the Wagner "A" mold), most American cast-iron Bundt-style pans were produced in the "traditional" style. Until recently, the last of the mass-produced, cast-iron Bundt pans manufactured in the US was the "Lodge Traditional Style Fluted Cake Pan," which ceased production in 2001 after more than fifty years on the market.

The lack of availability of new cast-iron Bundt pans in the US drove up the prices of used Bundt pans and created a robust collectible market for them. The market then got supercharged when these pans became widely available on online marketplaces such as eBay, Etsy, and, most recently, the collectibles groups on Facebook.

Then, in 2018, everything abruptly changed. A series of events combined to send the prices of cast-iron collectible Bundt pans into a free fall:

- **Competition:** Savvy European dealers, who have access to many of the most desirable cast-iron gugelhupfs in Europe, began selling their pans online to collectors in the US. The high prices that American collectors would pay for these pans created a fierce competition among these dealers. This eventually led them to start undercutting each other's prices. This competition caused the price of these pans to fall dramatically.
- **The Lodge Legacy Series Fluted Cake Pan:** In 2018, Lodge reintroduced an updated version of their "Fluted Style Cake Pan" as part of their "Legacy Series." At a price point of $70, it was a high-quality cast-iron Bundt pan priced lower than prices of similar collectible pans on the market. The Lodge Legacy pan also came preseasoned, so it was "ready to use" right out of the box, making it easy for noncollectors to easily get started baking with their cast-iron Bundt pan right away. The Lodge Legacy was available for only one year but ended up getting reintroduced again at the end of 2022, with a retail price of $79.95.
- **Carolina Cooker® Fluted Cast-Iron Cake Pan:** As if the Lodge Legacy wasn't tempting enough, another cast-iron Bundt pan entered the market, adding to the chaos. The Carolina Cooker® Bundt has a swirl-style design resembling the "Vater Brinkhouse" gugelhupf and comes preseasoned. Because the "Carolina Cooker" is manufactured in Shenzhen, China, where labor and material costs are lower than in the US, it can be ordered online for as low as $33!
- **Nordic Ware, Inc.:** To pour more gas on the fire, Nordic Ware has continued to flood the market with high-quality aluminum Bundt® pans, with amazing designs, priced in the $40–$60 range. Not only are the Nordic Ware pans well designed and inexpensive, but cast aluminum is much lighter and more nonstick than cast iron, making these pans more attractive to the majority of the households in the US than the heavier, more-difficult-to-use cast-iron Bundt pans.

While the last few years have been a dumpster fire for dealers of collectible cast-iron Bundt pans in the US, there has never been a better time as a buyer to begin collecting cast-iron cake pans. There are just a few things you should know before diving in.

## Buying Tips

If you have gotten this far, you are more than likely willing to forgo the benefits of modern, low-priced cast-iron or aluminum Nordic Ware Bundt® pans in favor of good old-fashioned collectible cast iron. If you are just getting started, here are some tips for buying these pans online.[13]

- If you frequent Facebook, you will find a multitude of cast-iron groups, including some that are dedicated to Bundt cakes and the buying and selling of cast-iron pans. You will learn a lot by becoming a member of these groups and reading through their posts. Most groups have archives going back several years.
- If you locate a particular pan when shopping online, look for recommendations from past buyers. Whether it is on eBay, Etsy, or a Facebook group, reading feedback from past customers is well worth your while.

- Look for clear photos without any blurring, weird lighting, or other colors layered onto the photo. Blurry photos can disguise possible casting flaws or damage that may impact the usability and value of a pan.
- If an item is listed in "as found" condition, it should be offered at a discount. Years of crud on an "as found" pan could be covering up cracks or holes, so be careful.
- Ask the seller about their return policy and who will pay shipping if an "old" crack is found. Trying to put the blame on the post office is not only immoral, but it is also illegal.
- When making a purchase from a Facebook group, look for a seller who is active in the forums beyond just selling. These folks are concerned about their reputation.
- Another piece of advice if making a purchase through a Facebook group is to pay using only PayPal "Goods & Services." The PayPal Goods & Services option includes insurance in case you do not receive your item in the mail, or if it arrives damaged or not as advertised. Note: You do not have to do this for purchases made on eBay or Etsy; insurance is automatically provided.
- Tracking information should be provided no more than three days after payment.
- When you receive your Bundt pan, rap the outside of the pan with your knuckles as soon as you take it out of the box, to see if it is cracked or otherwise damaged. It should ring like a bell. Make sure to do this in numerous places around the circumference of the Bundt pan just to be sure. Also hold the pan up to a bright light. This can help you spot any holes. I also recommend filling the pan with water, which can also help you identify any hidden holes. If you fill the pan to the top using a 1-cup measuring cup, this has the added benefit of providing the volume of the pan, which is helpful when adjusting your cake recipes to the size of your new Bundt pan.
- If there are any issues, contact the seller immediately. If you can't come to any sort of agreement, contact PayPal, eBay, or Etsy, and they will assist you in resolving any outstanding issues.
- Do not be afraid to share your purchase experience with others, both positive and negative. This helps build community and keeps everyone honest.
- Lastly, I find I get the best prices in the Facebook groups and on Facebook Marketplace, followed by eBay and then Etsy. I try to use eBay and Etsy only when they have an extremely rare item for sale that I have not been able to find on Facebook.

## Marked Pans

Marked pans enable collectors to easily identify the foundry where the pan originated. This also makes it easy to determine the age and value of the pan. Marks can come in the form of a foundry name, foundry mark, and numbers or letters (or both). Marks can have different meanings depending on the foundry.

Most of the collectible Bundt pans in the US were cast after 1950 and contain foundry names or marks or are at least well documented.

The same can't be said for European gugelhupf pans. The vast majority of cast-iron gugelhupf pans were unmarked. This makes it very difficult to identify the original foundries where they were cast. Complicating this is that many foundries in the region were converted to manufacture military goods during WWI and WWII. These foundries became military targets, and many were destroyed by the Allied armies in the first half of the twentieth century, along with their product catalogs, brochures, patterns, molds, and other items that would have helped identify the makers of these pans.

Luckily for collectors, a few of the most collectible gugelhupfs contain makers' marks, and significant progress has been made in recent years researching and identifying these marks and matching them to their respective foundries.

## Foundry Marks

Here are some examples of popular gugelhupf foundry marks.

**Gugelhupf Foundry Marks**

Carl Gottbill sel. Erben   Frank'sche Eisenwerk   Eisenwerk Lauchhammer

## Foundry Numbers and Letters

Foundries would mark pans with numbers and letters to help identify pans in their catalogs. On some pans, such as the Frank'sche Eisenwerk traditional-style gugelhupf pans, the "22 1/2" and the "25 1/2" marks denote the diameter of the pan.

Frank'sche 22 1/2 gugelhupf

Frank'sche 25 1/2 gugelhupf

Collectible Market  **17**

In other pans the number can reference the item number in the foundry's catalog or the number of the pattern, while the letter most likely refers to the mold used for casting the pan.

Some Bundt pans and gugelhupfs contain maker's marks, numbers, and letters. A good example of this is the fully marked Griswold 965 A65 fluted cake pan.

This example is marked "THE GRISWOLD MFG CO. ERIE, PA, CAKE MOLD," with a "965" being the pattern or part number and "A65" most likely being the mold used to cast the pan.

## Custom Foundry Marks

Some foundries in Europe offered an option to customize a gugelhupf pan with the buyer's initials on it. The most-common pans were the "Twister" swirl-style pan and the traditional-style gugelhupf with "propeller" handles.[14]

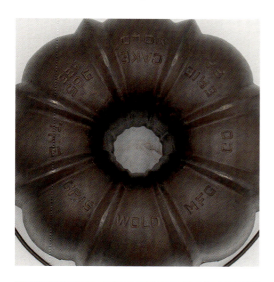

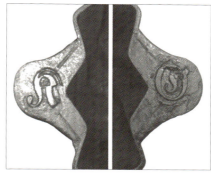

## Owner's Marks

Quite a few gugelhupf pans also contain marks made by their owners. These could be in the form of grind marks in the handles or edges of the pan, numbers or initials scratched on the outside of pans and handles, or metal tags attached to the handles.

In the second half of the nineteenth century, it was not uncommon for there to be communal bakeries in many French and German villages. Villagers would come together to bake bread and cakes in one large communal oven. Sometimes dozens of similar gugelhupfs would be together in an oven at the same time. According to Marc Wissen, a well-known German dealer in gugelhupf pans, it is believed that these owner's marks were identifiers that would ensure that everyone would get their own pan back when they were finished baking in the communal oven.[15]

# Dating Unmarked Pans

If a cast-iron Bundt pan you are interested in comes from an unknown maker, there are clues you can look for to get an idea of the pan's age. Understanding how the cast-iron manufacturing process has evolved over time is key to dating these pans.

## Sprue Marks and Gate Marks

Cast-iron cookware is manufactured through a method called "sand casting." The process begins with the creation of a "pattern" for a particular pan. A "mold" is then created by filling a wooden box with a damp, sand-based mixture and packing it around the pattern. The pattern is then removed, leaving a hollow space, or mold, in the shape of the desired pan. The pattern is used repeatedly to create many molds.

Molten iron is then poured into the mold and allowed to cool and solidify. Once it has cooled completely, the mold is broken, revealing the newly created cast-iron pan. This process requires that a new mold be made for each new pan. This is where the phrase "they broke the mold when they made that one" comes from. Because of the casting process, every cast-iron pan is unique in small and subtle ways.

All pans forged in this manner are left with a "casting mark," which is a rough area where the molten iron was either poured through holes directly into the mold cavity or flowed, through channels in the sand, into the mold.[16]

In the second half of the 1800s the most common method of sand casting was to pour the iron directly into the mold through what are known as "sprue holes." After the pan cooled and was removed from the mold, "sprue marks" would be left on the bottom of the pan. These marks would then be ground smooth so the pan would sit (relatively) flat, but the original round sprue marks would still be visible.

At some point during the late 1800s and into the early 1900s (depending on the country and the foundry), the method of sand casting began to evolve. Instead of pouring the molten iron through sprue holes into the mold, the hole evolved into long, thin channels. This facilitated a faster pour and better distribution of the molten iron into the mold cavity, reducing the number of defective castings. The channels would create "gate marks," which later would also be ground smooth but are also still visible as straight lines on the bottom of the pan.[17]

Sprue marks

Gate marks

Later casting evolved further still, with the molten iron poured into a mold from channels on the side. This moved the gate mark from the bottom to the lip, or edge, of a pan. This could then easily be ground smooth, leaving almost no casting marks whatsoever on the pan.

These date ranges are generalities, but looking for sprue marks and gate marks on the bottom of a Bundt pan is a good way to tell if a pan is old. If there are no sprue marks or gate marks, then the Bundt pan was most likely manufactured after 1950.

## Handles

Another way to get an idea of the age and origin of a Bundt pan is to look at its handles.

In the mid- to late 1800s, a gugelhupf, if it had handles, most likely would have had them welded on after the casting process. This proved inefficient and costly.

Later, as foundries modernized and automated as much of the manufacturing process as possible to reduce costs, handles were incorporated into the mold to bypass this time-consuming and costly last step.

**Welded handle**

**Molded handle**

So, while not an exact science by any means, inspecting an unmarked pan for clues such as sprue marks, gate marks, and welded handles can provide you with a rough idea of its age.

Handles can come in all shapes and sizes and, in many cases, can help identify the foundry that produced the pan. Most of the collectible American pans have unique handles that make them easy to identify.

**Griswold**       **J. C. Roberts**

 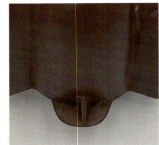

**Lodge "L"**      **Wagner "B"**

There are also many unknown gugelhupf pans that can be identified by their handle styles.

**Propeller**      **Bottle opener**

**Pierced ear**    **Fancy**

It is not uncommon to run across a pan with a small, vertical handle on it. The handle usually has a hole in it. At first glance it might seem to be too small to use as a handle for effectively lifting the pan, which is true. It is not intended to be a handle, but rather an anchor point for either a bail or a ring handle. In many cases the owner probably found the bails or rings cumbersome and simply removed them, leaving only the anchor point remaining.

There are some pans floating around that have vertical tab handles with no holes. Some have a very rough cast and look to be a recast of either a bail-handled or a ring-handled pan.

As a general rule, bailed-handle pans tend to originate from the US, and ring-handled pans tend to originate in Germany. One exception is the bailed "Ring Cake Pan with Tart Case Lid" gugelhupf that can be ordered new from Petromax in Germany.

## Enameled Pans

Enamel has been used on cast-iron cookware since the 1920s. While it's not something seen in collectible Bundt pans produced in the US, the opposite is true of collectible gugelhupf pans, especially ones from the eastern regions of Germany, the Czech Republic, and Poland. Because of this, collectors of gugelhupf pans know that if an unknown pan had been enameled, it was most likely cast in the 1920s or later and likely originated from one of these three countries.

The use of enameled cookware can be traced back to Eduard Bartelmus, a Czech chemist and inventor who was of German nationality. In the early 1830s he made the discovery of environmentally healthful enamel that did not release any poisonous heavy metals. This made it ideal for the production of enameled metal kitchenware.[18]

One of the benefits of enameled cast iron is that it does not require seasoning. In the early 1920s, enameling became very popular in gugelhupfs, in particular because, especially on the interior of the pan, the enamel provided a superior nonstick cooking surface when compared to a bare cast-iron gugelhupf.

In addition, enamel gives a cast-iron pan a more upscale look when compared to that of a bare cast-iron pan. The exterior and interior could be enameled in any color, in stark contrast to the dull-gray look of bare cast iron.[19]

Ironically, "upscale" enameled gugelhupfs typically hold a lower value as collectibles in the US than bare iron, since the enamel is often stained, cracked, or chipped. Unfortunately, this tends to make many enameled gugelhupfs better suited for display than for baking.[20]

# Pan Styles

## Traditional Style

This is the most common cake pan design, especially in the United States. This is primarily due to the Northland Bundt® pan made so famous by Ella Helfrich and her famous "Tunnel of Fudge" cake. The most collectible traditional-style Bundt pans are the fully marked Griswold "965" and Wagner's "B" mold pans, both originating in the US.

### Examples of "Traditional"-Style Cake Pans

Griswold "965"

Wagner "B"

Gottbill #2

Ring handles

## Crown Style

"Crown"-style gugelhupf pans have been interpreted by collectors to be patterned after the crowns of the European aristocracy, most likely because gugelhupf cakes were popularized by aristocrats in Europe, including Marie Antoinette of France and her nephew, Emperor Franz Joseph of the Austrian Empire. Crown-style pans are still very popular in Europe, particularly in Germany. The only known crown-style pan from the US is the Wagner "A" mold, which is patterned after the Gottbill Ironworks' "Royal Prince." The most collectible crown-style pan (and the most collectible of all cast-iron gugelhupf pans) is the German "Princess" from the "Triple Crown" series. Only three Princesses are currently known to exist.

### Examples of "Crown"-Style Cake Pans

Gottbill "Royal King"

Gottbill "Royal Queen"

Gottbill "Royal Prince"

The "Princess"

## Fluted Style

The Alsace region of France has had a strong influence on the fluted design. Most fluted pans originated in Europe, with the notable exceptions of the American "Hubcap" from Savery & Company and the "Fruit Top Pan" from the John Wright Company. The most collectible fluted style tube pan is the German "Cathedral."

### Examples of "Fluted"-Style Cake Pans

The "Cathedral"

The "Carnival"

Unknown fluted pan

Washington cake pan

## Swirl Style

Swirl-style Bundt pans (sometimes known as "Turks Head" pans) have fluted designs that are twisted to create a swirl pattern and are very sought after among cast-iron collectors. Only one collectible cast-iron swirl pan, known as the "Pilgrim," was made in the US. Most were produced in Germany.

### Examples of "Swirl"-Style Bundt Pans

The "Twister"

The "Hurricane"

The "Cyclone"

The "Pilgrim"

# Named Pans

While tremendous progress has been made identifying unknown European gugelhupf pans, there are still more than fifty collectible gugelhupfs whose foundries remain unknown. Not knowing the foundry or not having any identifying marks on a gugelhupf makes it difficult to identify. For this reason, many of the most popular unknown gugelhupfs now have well-established "names" that have been assigned them by the collector community.

So while in the US a known Bundt pan can be simply referred to as a Griswold "965," a Lodge "L" handle, or a Wagner "A Mold," many of the most popular unknown European gugelhupfs have been given names such as the "Cathedral" and the "Princess," enabling collectors to immediately identify a specific unknown pan. The naming of these pans is not popular with all collectors. Ideally, these names are a "stopgap" measure that has been put in place until the foundries that produced these unknown pans can be identified. For that reason, I have included the given names of these unknown pans in the descriptions where applicable.

## "Triple Crown" Series

The "Triple Crown" series is a nine-pan series of European gugelhupf cake forms named by the collector community that groups together a series of the most-collectible crown-style pans. All the gugelhupfs in the series are from unknown foundries and have no identifiable maker's marks. The "Triple Crown" series includes gugelhupfs known as the "Adelaide," the "Duchess," the "Excelsior," the "Grand Duke," the "King," the "Monarch," the "Prince," the "Princess," and the "Queen."

*Top left*: **The Queen**
*Top middle*: **The Grand Duke**
*Top right*: **The King**

*Bottom left*: **The Prince**
*Bottom right*: **The "Monarch" from the "Triple Crown" series**

25

# Known Collectible Bundt and Gugelhupf Pans

## Berkley Machine Works & Foundry Company (Norfolk, Virginia)

### Fig 1. The "Pilgrim" Swirl Style Cake Pan

**Width:** 10.5 in. / 26.7 cm
**Height:** 3.75 in. / 9.5 cm
**Weight:** 11.3 lbs. / 5.13 kg
**Volume:** 6 cups
**Value:** $250–$350
**Rarity:** ★★★★

**Description**
Swirl-style pan with flat tab handles. Swirls tighten dramatically as they reach the interior tube of the pan. Extremely rare pan cast at the Berkley Machine Works in Norfolk, Virginia, which makes this one of only two cast iron swirl-style Bundt pans produced. Ca. 1970. (USA)

### The Story behind the "Pilgrim"

Besides being the only known swirl-style pan cast in the US, the "Pilgrim" has an interesting history. A foundry worker at the Berkley Machine Works in Norfolk, Virginia, named Alfred Duncan borrowed an aluminum swirl pan from a family member and used it as a pattern for the pan (the origin and age of the pattern are unknown). "Pilgrim" pans were then cast "on the side," using the foundry's furnace during nonwork hours. Because of this, the "Pilgrim" pans were never listed as an official product of the foundry.

Alfred Duncan died in 1995, but his family still has the original pattern and one of the few known examples of one of Alfred Duncan's cast-iron "Pilgrims." His family believes that the pans were cast in the early 1970s and that very few pans were made. To date, less than ten are known to exist.

Given the circumstances around how the "Pilgrim" pans were cast, it is no surprise that out of the few examples known to exist, four variations of the Pilgrim are known. Three are related to the handles on the pan: three have solid handles (like the pattern), the fourth has a handle with one hole in it, and the fifth has holes in both handles. One "Pilgrim" even has a solid tube.

Gwen Duncan holding her family's aluminum pattern and a cast-iron "Pilgrim"[21]

# Buzuluk a.s. (Komárov, Czech Republic)

Buzuluk a.s. is one of the oldest foundries in the world. Originally called the "Komárovské železárny" (Komárov Ironworks), it was established in 1460 in the town of Komárov, about 30 miles west of Prague, in what is now the Czech Republic.

At one point in the nineteenth century, under the rule of the Prince of Hanau family, the Komárov Ironworks foundry was one of the largest foundries in the entire Austrian Empire.[22]

In 1879, Komárov began production of round wood-burning stoves, army cannonballs, pots, pans, and other commercial cookware.[23]

Komárov Ironworks continued production throughout the twentieth century. In 1948 the company was nationalized by the government and in 1949 was renamed Buzuluk Komárov National Corporation. With the fall of communism in eastern Europe, the Buzuluk Komárov National Corporation was privatized and renamed simply "Buzuluk a.s."

In 2012, Buzuluk a.s. was acquired by a Chinese-owned corporation called Dalian. Current manufacturing focuses not on cast-iron production, but rather on manufacturing rubber-processing machinery and piston rings as their core business.

While the primary focus of the Buzuluk foundry has evolved over the years, they have continued their tradition of "art casting." The forging process is still done entirely by hand and according to old techniques. The local Komárov

Original cast-iron cookware on display at the Komárovské (Buzuluk) museum in Komárov, Czech Republic

Museum in Komárov contains many examples of popular unmarked gugelhupf pans, or "babovka" pans, as they are called in the Czech Republic. On display are examples of what American collectors have named the "Dolman," the "Duchess," the "Lady," the "Lotus Flower," and the "Turban." In addition, many popular and collectible shallow cake forms cast by Buzuluk are also on display.

With the acquisition of Buzuluk by Dalian, Buzuluk ceased selling their pans directly to customers. Instead, they signed a production contract with Český smalt sro, another Czech company specializing in enameled cookware. Buzuluk provides Český smalt with their line of raw cast-iron cookware, which is then enameled and marketed by Český smalt under the name "Gourmetina."[24] These can be purchased new in the Czech Republic at retail stores or online.[25]

Nonenameled Buzuluk patterns continue to be manufactured, though the source of these pans is unknown. It has been speculated that access inventory manufactured at Buzuluk, originally intended for Český smalt (and therefore not enameled), makes its way to local markets in the Czech Republic. These eventually find their way to dealers in Europe, who then sell them to collectors in the United States.

In 2020, Buzuluk discontinued the production of all their cast-iron pans to focus on their core business of manufacturing rubber-processing machinery and piston rings. The "Gourmetina" line of cast-iron enameled pans, which still use some of the original Komárovské železárny (Buzuluk) patterns, is still available, though production is now outsourced by Český smalt to a different foundry in the Czech Republic.

## Buzuluk a.s.

### Fig 1. The "Dolman" crown-style cake pan

**Width:** 9.8 in. / 25 cm
**Height:** 4.1 in. / 10.3 cm
**Weight:** 6.8 lbs. / 3.1 kg
**Volume:** 13 cups
**Value:** $200–$275
**Rarity:** ★ ★ ★

**Description**
Crown-style pan with a bubbletop on an elevated, ornate base. Very common. Frequently found with enameled interior and exterior. Produced by the Komárov Ironworks (Czech Republic).

## Buzuluk a.s.

### Fig 2. The "Duchess" Pattern Crown Style Cake Pan
### (Triple Crown Series)

 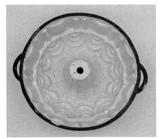  

**Width:** 10.2 in. / 25.9 cm
**Height:** 3.5 in. / 8.9 cm
**Weight:** 6.6 lbs. / 3 kg
**Volume:** 9 cups
**Value:** $250–$350
**Rarity:** ★ ★ ★

**Description**
Crown-style pan with five stacked arches atop an ornate base. Often found with enameled interior. Sometimes marked with the number "8." Frequently gets confused with the "Dominion," which has four stacked arches atop an elevated, ornate base. Part of the "Triple Crown" series. Produced by the Komárov Ironworks (Czech Republic).

34  COLLECTIBLE CAST IRON

## Buzuluk a.s.

### Fig 3. The "Lady" Crown Style Cake Pan

**Width:** 8.8 in. / 22.3 cm
**Height:** 4.4 in. / 11.2 cm
**Weight:** 5.5 lbs. / 2.45 kg
**Volume:** 13 cups
**Value:** $200–$275
**Rarity:** ★ ★ ★

**Description**
Crown-style gugelhupf with teardrop-shaped bubbletop mounted on a tall, ornate base with molded handles. Frequently found with enamel interior and exterior. Close resemblance to the Dolman. Produced by the Komárov Ironworks (Czech Republic).

## Buzuluk a.s.

### Fig 4. The "Lotus Flower" Cake Pan

**Width:** 10.0 in. / 25.4 cm
**Height:** 5.2 in. / 13.2 cm
**Weight:** 9.4 lbs. / 4.3 kg
**Volume:** 11.5 cups
**Value:** $250–$300
**Rarity:** ★ ★ ★

**Description**
Unmarked and appears to be twenty-first century. Alternating layered lotus leaves on top of a flat base with welded-on, fancy handles. Produced by the Komárov Ironworks (Czech Republic).

## Buzuluk a.s.

### Fig 5. "Big Bake Mold" Traditional Style Cake Pan

 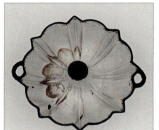  

**Width:** 10.25 in. / 26 cm
**Height:** 4.33 in. / 11 cm
**Weight:** 6.4 lbs. / 2.9 kg
**Volume:** 14 cups
**Value:** $100–$150
**Rarity:** ★ ★

**Description**
Traditional-style pan with molded handles and a smooth tube. Can be found with a white enamel interior and colored enameled exterior. Produced by the Buzuluk foundry in the Czech Republic.

Known Collectible Bundt and Gugelhupf Pans 37

## Buzuluk a.s.

### Fig 6. "Small Bake Mold" Traditional Style Cake Pan

**Width:** 7.9 in. / 20 cm
**Height:** 3.5 in. / 9 cm
**Weight:** 6.4 lbs. / 2.9 kg
**Volume:** 7 cups
**Value:** $100–$150
**Rarity:** ★ ★

**Description**
Swirl-style pan with molded handles and a smooth tube. Can be found in white with enamel interior and colored enameled exterior. Produced by the Buzuluk foundry in the Czech Republic.

## Buzuluk a.s.

### Fig 7. The "Turban" Crown Style Ring Cake Pan

**Width:** 10.9 in. / 27.8 cm
**Height:** 2.95 in. / 7.5 cm
**Weight:** 6.5 lbs. / 2.95 kg
**Volume:** 9 cups
**Value:** $275–$375
**Rarity:** ★ ★ ★

**Description**
Vintage ring cake mold with top swirl and molded handles. Produced by the Buzuluk foundry in the Czech Republic.

# Cousances-Le Creuset (Cousances-les-Forges, France)

Les Hauts Fourneaux Cousances was a French cookware manufacturer known for enameled cast-iron pans (*cocottes* in French). The Cousances foundry, in Cousances-les-Forges in northeastern France, began making cast-iron pans in 1553 and by the mid-twentieth century was a major competitor of Le Creuset.

In 1957, Le Creuset bought out Cousances, acquiring its patterns and adopting the highly regarded Cousances designs. The original Cousances designs are still produced today by Le Creuset from the original patterns in the original foundry/factory.

Le Creuset has changed the colors of the cookware in the old Cousances patterns, but original Cousances pots, pans, skillets, roasters, and Dutch ovens are still to be found as used pieces and are recognizable by the medallion logo. The newer Cousances designs feature glazed natural-color cast-iron bottoms, which they share with the Le Creuset current line, and are marked "Cousances–Made in France."

Cookware under the Cousances brand continued to be manufactured by Le Creuset into the early 1980s.[26] Today, Le Creuset has grown into an international brand with a product range that spans various categories, including cast iron, stainless steel, stoneware, nonstick, and dinnerware. Le Creuset is now sold in more than sixty countries around the world, including the US, UK, Japan, and Australia.[27]

*Images courtesy Le Creuset*

## Cousances-Le Creuset

### Fig 1. Fluted-Style Cake Pan—Marked

**Width:** 9.1 in. / 23.1 cm
**Height:** 3.9 in. / 9.8 cm
**Weight:** 4.7 lbs. / 2.1 kg
**Volume:** 12 cups
**Value:** $125–$175
**Rarity:** ★ ★

**Description**
French "kouglof" pan marked "Cousances" and "Made in France." One of the molded handles has a hole in it for hanging. Produced by Le Creuset. (France)

# Eisenwerk Lauchhammer (Lauchhammer-Ost, Germany)

The Eisenwerk Lauchhammer was founded in 1725 by the Baroness of Löwendal. The "Lauch-Hammer" foundry was named after the ponds and lakes nearby. The foundry was built with a charcoal blast furnace adjacent to extensive bog iron ore deposits located on her land. After she died in 1776, the baroness's art-loving heir, Detlev Carl von Einsiedel, took over the foundry and focused production on cast iron and bronze art casting.[28]

During the nineteenth century, the foundry expanded and began producing cast-iron furniture and other everyday objects. These items included cast-iron bathtubs, pissoirs (public urinals), public water fountains, pipes, cigar cutters, lighters, and pots and pans, including gugelhupf pans. The bathtubs, pissoires, and pots and pans were made from cast iron and contained enamel interiors.

In the early twentieth century, the foundry became a major provider of fine bronze statues. Production at Lauchhammer had to be stopped for the duration of the First World War. After the war, Lauchhammer began producing bronze bells. Between 1920 and 1939, approximately five hundred bells were produced and were sent all over the world. During the period of Nazi rule from 1933 to 1944, the foundry produced mainly National Socialist art, from large sculptures to plaques.[29]

The initial Lauchhammer foundry mark was created in 1872 and used until 1921. The mark contains a raised field with a hammer and mallet, and above them the crown of counts of the von Einsiedel family.[30]

A cast-iron Lauchhammer gugelhupf pan with an enamel interior is on display in the Kunstgussmuseum Lauchhammer.[31]

The foundry still exists today as Lauchhammer Kunstguss and is known primarily for their artistic bronze castings.

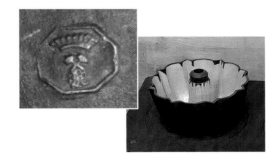

## Eisenwerk Lauchhammer

### Fig 1. Traditional-Style Cake Pan—Marked

**Width:** 10.6 in. / 26.9 cm
**Height:** 5.1 in. / 13 cm
**Weight:** 8.2 lbs. / 3.7 kg
**Volume:** 16 cups
**Value:** $100–$150
**Rarity:** ★ ★ ★ ★ ★

**Description**
Traditional-style gugelhupf with the "Lauchhammer" mark and the number "9." Double gate marked with enameled interior. Crude cast, possibly a recast. (Germany)

Known Collectible Bundt and Gugelhupf Pans 43

# Eisenwerk Lauchhammer

## Fig 2. "Duchess" Pattern Crown Style Cake Pan—Marked

**Width:** 10.8 in. / 27.4 cm
**Height:** 4.3 in. / 10.9 cm
**Weight:** 6.3 lbs. / 2.87 kg
**Volume:** 9 cups
**Value:** $250–$350
**Rarity:** ★ ★ ★ ★

**Description**
Handled crown-style pan based on the "Duchess" pattern. Marked with the "Lauchhammer" mark and the number "8." Crude cast, possibly a recast of "the Duchess" from Buzuluk. (Germany)

## Eisenwerk Lauchhammer

### Fig 3. "Duchess Wolfe" Pattern Swirl Style Cake Pan—Marked

**Width:** 8.3 in. / 21 cm
**Height:** 4.7 in. / 12 cm
**Weight:** 4.2 lbs. / 1.9 kg
**Volume:** 8 cups
**Value:** $200–$250
**Rarity:** ★★★★

**Description**

Swirl-style pan based on the "Duchess Wolfe" pattern. Displays the "Lauchhammer" mark and the number "6." Gate marked, and like all Lauchhammer gugelhupf pans, it comes with an enameled interior. Unrestored pan in as-found condition. (Germany)

# Eisenwerk Martinlamitz GmbH
# (Schwarzenbach an der Saale, Germany)

The Martinlamitz hammer mill is located outside Schwarzenbach, on the Saale River near the Czech border. The earliest mention of the "hammer mill" goes back as far as 1200, making it one of the oldest continuously operating foundries in Europe. In 1390, the Martinlamitz community consisted of a hammer mill, a mill, a smithy, and ten farms.[32]

The Martinlamitz hammer mill was incorporated as a public company under the name "Eisenwerk Martinlamitz AG" in 1920. The foundry burned down shortly afterward but was quickly rebuilt. The foundry fell on hard times during the global Great Depression, declaring bankruptcy in 1929.[33]

The foundry was then reorganized as a private company under the name Eisenwerk Martinlamitz GmbH in 1932. The company is still operational today and now employs 450 people. The foundry produces cast-iron parts for railway, construction, vehicles, engineering, hydraulics, and agricultural industries. They have customers in twenty-one countries around the world, including Korea, India, and China.[34]

## Eisenwerk Martinlamitz GmbH

### Fig 1. Traditional-Style Cake Pan—Marked

**Width:** 5.1 in. / 13 cm
**Height:** 10.2 in. / 26 cm
**Weight:** 8.2 lbs. / 3.7 kg
**Volume:** 17 cups
**Value:** $100–$150
**Rarity:** ★★★★★

**Description**
Ca. 1932. Traditional-style, handled gugelhupf, with oxblood-red-enameled exterior and white-enameled interior. Double gate marked on the bottom of the pan. Displays the "Eisenwerk Martinlamitz" " foundry mark. One example is known to exist. (Germany)

# Frank'sche Eisenwerk GmbH, Adolfshütte (Hesse, Germany)

Christian Frank (April 28, 1787–July 5, 1851) studied theology as a young man and eventually succeeded his father as pastor in Vöhl, Germany, in 1812. Christian, who had many liberal ideas, eventually came into conflict with the state government in Darmstadt. In 1834, his liberal leanings led to him being transferred to an insufficiently endowed pastor's post in Hatzfeld, Germany. To create a better livelihood for himself and his family, on April 29, 1839, Christian Frank, along with his younger brother Georg Frank, and another partner, Carl Giebeler, purchased the Niederscheld hammer mill under the name of "Frank & Giebeler oHG."

After the death of George Frank in 1850 and the departure of Carl Giebeler in 1897, the Frank family completely owned the company. On May 1, 1897, "Frank & Giebeler oHG" was transformed into a family company operating under the name Frank'sche Eisenwerk GmbH, Adolfshütte. Eisenwerk later became famous for their "Oranier" ovens and at one point had more than three thousand employees.

During World War I, many employees were drafted into the military. The company was able to remain running by employing women, which was unheard of at the time.

After WWI the foundry struggled. At the end of 1931, all production of cast-iron cookware was halted. From 1931 onward, the Frank'sche Eisenwerk foundry focused solely on manufacturing their famous "Oranier" stoves.[35]

During World War II the company manufactured ovens, field kitchens, bullet casings, and other war-essential products for the Wehrmacht. In addition, they also manufactured parts for the Heinkel-Jäger He 162, the German single-engine, jet-powered fighter aircraft flown by the Luftwaffe. Unfortunately, this made the Frank'sche Eisenwerk a prime military target, and most of the factory was destroyed by Allied bombings on February 25 and 28, 1945.[36] Following World War II the foundry focused on manufacturing accessories for oil and gas stoves but never again manufactured cast-iron cookware.

## Frank'sche Eisenwerk GmbH, Adolfshütte

### Fig 1. Traditional-Style Cake Pan—Marked "Frank" & "22 ½"

**Width:** 8.6 in. / 22.5 cm
**Height:** 4.3 in. / 11 cm
**Weight:** 5.7 lbs. / 2.6 kg
**Volume:** 15 cups
**Value:** $100–$150
**Rarity:** ★★★★

**Description**
Traditional-style gugelhupf, double gate marked with welded-on handles. Displays the "Frank" maker's mark as well as a "22 ½," denoting the diameter of the pan. (Germany)

Known Collectible Bundt and Gugelhupf Pans **49**

# Frank'sche Eisenwerk GmbH, Adolfshütte

## Fig 2. Traditional-Style Cake Pan—Marked "Frank" & "25 ½"

**Width:** 10.0 in. / 25.5 cm
**Height:** 4.6 in. / 11.6 cm
**Weight:** 6.6 lbs. / 3.0 kg
**Volume:** 17 cups
**Value:** $100–$150
**Rarity:** ★★★

**Description**

Traditional-style gugelhupf, double gate marked with welded-on handles. Displays the "Frank" maker's mark as well as a "25 ½," denoting the diameter of the pan. (Germany)

## Frank'sche Eisenwerk GmbH, Adolfshütte

### Fig 3. "Queen" Pattern Crown Style Cake Pan—Marked

**Width:** 10.0 in. / 25.5 cm
**Height:** 4.8 in. / 12.3 cm
**Weight:** 8.2 lbs. / 3.7 kg
**Volume:** 19 cups
**Value:** $225–$325
**Rarity:** ★★★

**Description**

Queen-style crown pan with welded-on handles. Displays the "Frank" mark. Also marked with a "26," which denotes the width of the pan. Double gate marked. Identical design to the "Royal Queen" from the Crown Jewel series by Carl Gottbill sel. Erben foundry. Rougher cast and slightly smaller size suggests it could even be a recast of the Gottbill Royal Queen. (Germany)

# Gottbill sel Erben Eisenwerk (Mariahütte, Germany)

Gottbill Eisenwerk was founded by Carl Gottbill in 1715. The foundry was in Mariahütte, Germany. Upon his death in 1773, not having any sons, he bequeathed the foundry to his nephew, Carl II.

Carl II continued to successfully grow the business and greatly expanded the foundry. This growth continued when his son, Carl III, took over running the foundry after the death of his father in 1856. He built a second foundry, originally called the Nonnweiler Hütte, which he piously placed under the protection of the Mother of God, and therefore christened the foundry "MariaHütte." Under his leadership, the two foundries of the Gottbill Eisenwerk became widely recognized throughout Germany.

Carl III and his wife, Catharina Doell, had seven children, including five sons. All five of the sons became smelters. Because of this, the foundry was later renamed Carl Gottbill sel. Erben (Carl Gottbill and Heirs). Despite having such a large family, none of the sons had any children, which eventually ended the Gottbill family line.[37]

The foundry then passed through several different owners, continuing into the twentieth century. Following World War I, production collapsed. The foundry started manufacturing cast parts and furnaces (stoves, ovens, and oil ovens) to add to their product line. These additional products, combined with the beginning of the rearmament of Germany in the 1930s, brought the foundry back to life, renamed as GOMA (GOttbill MAriahuette).

During World War II, the Gottbill Eisenwerk supplied the German armed forces primarily with field-cooking stoves. Luckily, they were spared any bombing or damage during the war. At the end of the 1950s, furnace production gradually decreased, and the company was bought by Diehl in 1960.[38]

Following World War II the foundry manufactured everything from commercial items such as rod irons and cutting dies, to household items such as oil lamps, handle kettles, pots, pans, and gugelhupf pans.

Until recently the Gottbill Eisenwerk was not on any collector's radar. Then a vintage, unused cast-iron oval roaster was purchased by a German collector that still had an original label attached to it. This discovery turned the cast-iron collector community upside down.

While most European cast-iron gugelhupfs are unmarked, there was one mark that was present on many of the most collectible cast-iron gugelhupf pans available in Germany.

For years this mark was thought to be a "LC," representing "Le Creuset." There were a couple of reasons why this was disputed by many collectors.

First, these pans were dated to the first half of the twentieth century—a time when France and Germany were not exactly on friendly terms. So it is unlikely that Germany was importing a significant amount of pans from France during this time.

Later, Marc Strümper, a well-known German collector and dealer, was able to contact the archivist at Le Creuset, who confirmed that the unknown logo was not one from the Le Creuset company.

The discovery of this label confirmed what many collectors believed all along—that these were not Le Creuset pans but that they came from a German foundry—the Carl Gottbill Eisenwerk.

Armed with this information, another collector located a product catalog from the Gottbill Eisenwerk from August 1933. It contained detailed information about cast-iron cookware from the Gottbill foundry for that year. The pans listed in the catalog coincided exactly with the found pans that contained these maker's marks. This was indisputable evidence confirming that these were in fact Gottbill pans, and not from Le Creuset.[39]

All the gugelhupfs listed in the catalog were offered in "rohguß" (raw cast iron) and in "inox dirt," a special heat treatment resulting in a bluish color that is rustproof, which Gottbill patented in 1883. Sometimes during the restoration process the bluish inox dirt exterior is revealed. Once regular seasoning is applied, the color disappears and the exterior looks like "raw" seasoned cast iron.

The following Carl Gottbill gugelhupf pans have well-established "names" created by the collector community as a way of identifying gugelhupf pans prior to the discovery of the Gottbill catalog. For the purposes of continuity, we will continue to use these names but will also reference the Gottbill catalog number of each marked pan.

Known Collectible Bundt and Gugelhupf Pans

## Gottbill sel Erben Eisenwerk

### Fig 1. Traditional Style Cake Pan–Marked "#1"

Fig. 18

**Width:** 8.9 in. / 25.5 cm
**Height:** 4.3 in. / 11 cm
**Weight:** 6.6 lbs. / 3.0 kg
**Volume:** 17 cups
**Value:** $100–$150
**Rarity:** ★★★

**Description**

Ca. 1933. Traditional-style gugelhupf. Contains the Gottbill maker's mark and is usually marked with a "1" pattern number. Sometimes also marked with a backward "C." Available with and without molded handles. Listed in a 1933 Gottbill catalog (fig. 18). (German)

## Gottbill sel Erben Eisenwerk

### Fig 2. Traditional Style Cake Pan–Marked "#2"

**Width:** 11.1 in. / 28.3 cm
**Height:** 4.6 in. / 11.7 cm
**Weight:** 11.0 lbs. / 5.0 kg
**Volume:** 13 cups
**Value:** $150–$200
**Rarity:** ★★★

**Description**
Ca. 1933. Traditional gugelhupf design on a flat base. Contains the Gottbill mark and is usually marked with a "2" pattern number. Listed in a 1933 Gottbill catalog (fig. 19). (German)

# Gottbill sel Erben Eisenwerk

## Fig 3. Fluted Shallow Cake Form

No known examples exist. There has been speculation that this may be the highly collectible "Oak Leaf" gugelhupf. However, the Gottbill catalog shows a shallow cake form with a tapered tube, without handles. Also the "Oak Leaf" is unmarked, and its dimensions differ from what is listed in the Gottbill catalog.

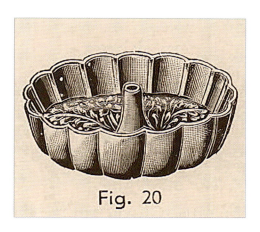

**Width:** 10.8 in. / 27.4 cm
**Height:** 2.5 in. / 6.4 cm
**Weight:** 8.8 lbs. / 4.0 kg
**Volume:** Unknown
**Value:** TBD
**Rarity:** N/A

**Description**

Ca. 1933. Shallow cake form depicting leaves and flowers. No known examples exist (German). Possibly the unmarked gugelhupf known as the "Oakleaf." Listed in the 1933 Gottbill catalog (fig. 20). (Germany)

# Gottbill sel Erben Eisenwerk

## Crown Jewel Series

The "Crown Jewel" series is a name given by the collector community to the four crown-style gugelhupf pans with the "Carl Gottbill sel Erben" maker's mark. They also correspond to the 1933 Carl Gottbill sel Erben catalog. Fig. 21 is the "Royal Prince," fig. 22 is the "Royal King," fig. 23 is the "Hoot," and fig. 24 is the "Royal Queen."

"Royal King," "Royal Queen," "Royal Prince," and the "Hoot" from the Gottbill Eisenwerk "Crown Jewel" series

Known Collectible Bundt and Gugelhupf Pans 57

# Gottbill sel Erben Eisenwerk

## Fig 4. The "Royal King" Crown Style Cake Pan—Marked

**Width:** 9.4 in. / 24.0 cm
**Height:** 4.7 in. / 12.0 cm
**Weight:** 6.6 lbs. / 3.0 kg
**Volume:** 16 1/2 cups
**Value:** $250–$350
**Rarity:** ★★★

**Description**
Ca. 1933. Crown-style gugelhupf, double gate marked with molded handles displaying the Gottbill Eisenwerk mark. Also commonly marked with a "24." Listed in a 1933 Gottbill catalog (fig. 22). (German)

## Gottbill sel Erben Eisenwerk

### Fig 5. The "Royal Queen" Crown Style Cake Pan–Marked

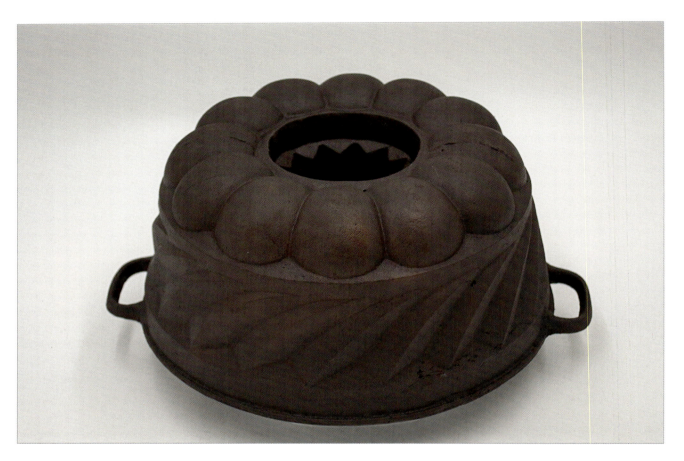

**Width:** 10.2 in. / 26.0 cm
**Height:** 5.0 in. / 12.7 cm
**Weight:** 7.7 lbs. / 3.5 kg
**Volume:** 21 cups
**Value:** $250–$350
**Rarity:** ★★★

**Description**
Ca. 1933. Crown-style Queen gugelhupf, double gate marked with molded handles displaying the Gottbill Eisenwerk mark. Also marked "26." Listed in a 1933 Gottbill catalog (fig. 24). (German)

Known Collectible Bundt and Gugelhupf Pans 59

## Gottbill sel Erben Eisenwerk

### Fig 6. The "Royal Prince"-Crown Style Cake Pan—Marked

**Width:** 8.7 in. / 22.0 cm
**Height:** 4.5 in. / 11.5 cm
**Weight:** 5.5 lbs. / 2.5 kg
**Volume:** 11 1/2 cups
**Value:** $200–$275
**Rarity:** ★★★

**Description**
Ca. 1933. Crown-style gugelhupf, double gate marked with molded handles displaying the Gottbill Eisenwerk mark. Also marked "#22." Comes with and without handles. Often confused with the Wagner "A" listed in a 1933 Gottbill catalog (fig. 21). (German)

## Gottbill sel Erben Eisenwerk

### Fig 7. The "Hoot"-Crown Style Cake Pan—Marked

**Width:** 9.8 in. / 25 cm
**Height:** 3.9 in. / 10 cm
**Weight:** 5 lbs. / 2.3 kg
**Volume:** 14 cups
**Value:** $200–$275
**Rarity:** ★ ★ ★

**Description**
Ca. 1933. Crown-style gugelhupf, double gate marked with molded handles displaying the Gottbill Eisenwerk mark. Also marked with a "25." Listed in a 1933 Gottbill catalog (fig. 23). (German)

Known Collectible Bundt and Gugelhupf Pans  61

## Gottbill sel Erben Eisenwerk

### Fig 8. The "Duchess Wolfe" Swirl Style Cake Pan—Marked

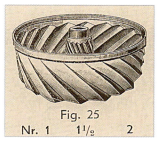

**Width:** 8.5 in. / 21.5 cm
**Height:** 2.9 in. / 7.30 cm
**Weight:** 4.1 lbs. / 1.85 kg
**Volume:** Unknown
**Value:** $150–$200
**Rarity:** ★ ★ ★ ★ ★

**Width:** 9.4 in. / 24.0 cm
**Height:** 4.8 in. / 12.2 cm
**Weight:** 6.6 lbs. / 3.00 kg
**Volume:** 10 cups

**Width:** 11.2 in. / 28.5 cm
**Height:** 4.9 in. / 12.5 cm
**Weight:** 9.9 lbs. / 4.50 kg
**Volume:** Unknown

**Description**
Ca. 1933. Comes in three sizes. Swirl-style pan, double gate marked with a spiral tube. Extremely rare. Listed in a 1933 Gottbill catalog (fig. 25).

Gottbill sel

## Erben Eisenwerk

### Fig 9. The "Cyclone"-Swirl Style Cake Pan–Marked

**Width:** 11.2 in. / 28.5 cm
**Height:** 5.1 in. / 12.9 cm
**Weight:** 9.4 lbs. / 4.27 kg
**Volume:** 24 cups
**Value:** $150–$200
**Rarity:** ★★★

**Description**
Ca. 1933. Crown-style gugelhupf, with the Gottbill Eisenwerk mark. Also marked "3" and "C" or "V." Double gate marked with a tall, plain tube. Listed in a 1933 Gottbill catalog (fig. 26). (German)

Known Collectible Bundt and Gugelhupf Pans **63**

## Gottbill sel Erben Eisenwerk

### Fig 10. Swirl Style Cake Pan–Marked

**Width:** 9.3 in. / 23.5 cm
**Height:** 3.5 in. / 8.8 cm
**Weight:** 4.4 lbs. / 2.0 kg
**Volume:** 6 cups

**Width:** 11.8 in. / 30 cm
**Height:** 3.7 in. / 9.5 cm
**Weight:** 8.3 lbs. / 3.75 kg
**Volume:** Unknown
**Value:** $150–$200
**Rarity:** ★★★★★

**Description**
Ca. 1933. Comes in three sizes. Swirl-style pan, double gate marked with a spiral tube. Only two Gottbill marked "Hurricanes" are known to exist. Both are in the "1 ½" marked middle size. One has handles, and one does not. Listed in a 1933 Gottbill catalog (fig. 25).

# Griswold Manufacturing Company

The Seldon-Griswold Manufacturing Company was an American manufacturer of cast-iron kitchen products founded in Erie, Pennsylvania, in 1865. The company was founded by Matthew Griswold and his cousins, brothers J. C. and Samuel Selden. In 1884, Matthew Griswold purchased the Selden family's interests. He then reorganized and chartered the company as the Griswold Manufacturing Company.

The company originally manufactured hinges, stovepipe dampers, thimbles, and other stove furniture. In the 1870s, Griswold began to manufacture skillets, pots, grinding mills, and waffle irons.[40]

Griswold developed an international reputation for manufacturing the highest-quality cast-iron cookware. Griswold brands included Selden & Griswold, Erie, Griswold's Erie, Griswold, Victor, Iron Mountain, Good Health, Best Made, Merit, and Puritan.[41]

By the 1940s the company was in financial difficulty, facing competition from manufacturers of more-modern products while struggling with internal labor disputes and declining quality.

In 1957, McGraw-Edison of Chicago, Illinois, acquired Griswold Manufacturing. Later that year, the Griswold brand and housewares division were sold to the Wagner Manufacturing Company of Sidney, Ohio. Shortly thereafter the plant in Erie closed, with sixty employees being laid off.[42]

Griswold manufactured a Bundt pan from 1910 to 1940. The pan was in the traditional style with a bailed handle and was marked "THE GRISWOLD MFG CO. ERIE, PA, CAKE MOLD, 965."

Griswold also manufactured an advertising pan for Frank W Hay & Sons. It was identical to Griswold's 965 cake pan, except the pan was marked "FRANK W HAY & SONS, JOHNSTOWN PA, PATD MARCH 10 1891."[43]

The scarcity and quality of Griswold cast-iron cookware have created a large community of collectors. The Griswold & Cast Iron Cookware Association (GCICA) is a collector organization with seven-hundred-plus members residing in the United States and Canada. For information regarding events and membership, go to www.gcica.org or visit their Facebook page.

# Griswold Manufacturing

## Fig 1. 965 Traditional-Style Fluted Bundt Pan—Marked

**Width:** 9.3 in. / 23.5 cm
**Height:** 4.3 in. / 11 cm
**Weight:** 5.7 lbs. / 2.6 kg
**Volume:** 14 cups
**Value:** $750–$1,000
**Rarity:** ★★

**Description**

Traditional-style Bundt with a bailed handle. (USA) Four variations exist:
- marked "THE GRISWOLD MFG CO. ERIE, PA, CAKE MOLD"
- marked "THE GRISWOLD MFG CO. ERIE, PA, CAKE MOLD" with a "965" for the pattern number
- marked "THE GRISWOLD MFG CO. ERIE, PA, CAKE MOLD" with a "965" and a "G"
- marked "THE GRISWOLD MFG CO. ERIE, PA, CAKE MOLD" with a "965" and a "A65" (pictured)

## Frank W Hay & Sons (Griswold)

### Fig 1. Traditional-Style Fluted Bundt Pan—Marked

**Width:** 9.3 in. / 23.5 cm
**Height:** 4.3 in. / 11 cm
**Weight:** 5.7 lbs. / 2.6 kg
**Volume:** 14 cups
**Value:** $450–$650
**Rarity:** ★★

**Description**

Advertising Bundt pan for Frank W Hay and Sons. Manufactured by Griswold. Identical to the Griswold traditional-style 965. (USA). Two variations:
- marked "FRANK W HAY & SONS, JOHNSTOWN PA, PATD MARCH 10 1891"
- marked "FRANK W HAY & SONS, JOHNSTOWN PA, PATD MARCH 10 1891" and the Griswold "965" pattern number. (*pictured*). Unrestored pan in as-found condition. (USA)

## J. C. Roberts

Primarily known for producing artistic bronze sculptures, the J. C. Roberts foundry was also known for producing cast-iron Bundt pans.

## J. C. Roberts

### Fig 1. Traditional-Style Bundt Pan—Marked

  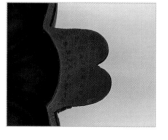 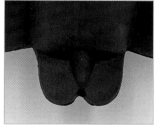

**Width:** 9.7 in. / 24.6 cm
**Height:** 4.5 in. / 11.5 cm
**Weight:** 9.9 lbs. / 4.5 kg
**Volume:** 14.5 cups
**Value:** $100–$150
**Rarity:** ★★

**Description**

Traditional-style pan. Easily identifiable by its reinforced, double-tabbed handles and its extra-long tube. Molded handles and side gated, which suggested it is a mid-twentieth-century Bundt pan. It is thought that these were used in bakeries, and the long tube allowed the pans to be stacked while baking in the oven. (USA)[46]

## John Wright Company

John Wright Company has been manufacturing souvenirs and gifts on the banks of the Susquehanna River in Wrightsville, Pennsylvania, since 1947. In the 1980s, when market trends shifted away from cast-iron toys and novelties, the John Wright Company began to focus on reproduction and shutter hardware. They also have branched out into steel and stainless-steel hardware products.

## John Wright Company

### Fig 1. Fruit Top Fluted-Style Bundt Pan—Marked

**Width:** 8.9 in. / 22.6 cm
**Height:** TBD
**Weight:** 5 lbs. / 2.3 kg
**Volume:** 6 cups
**Value:** $175–$250
**Rarity:** ★★

**Description**
Produced in 1984. Small mold, fruit top cake pan with fluted edges. (USA)
Four variations are known to exist:
- button that reads "Classic Gourmet" on the bottom of the pan
- button anchor spot, but no button attached (standard cast iron color)
- button anchor spot, but no button attached (dark cast-iron color)
- button anchor buttered over, "All-Clad®" finish

# Lodge Manufacturing Company

In 1896, Joseph Lodge started the Blacklock Foundry in South Pittsburg, Tennessee. The foundry was named after his longtime friend Joseph Hayton Blacklock, the minister at the local Episcopal church. The company was focused on manufacturing a wide range of cast-iron products, including cast-iron cookware and sad irons.

In May 1910, a fire destroyed the foundry. Just shortly after midnight, a fire reportedly started from the cupola. Since the buildings were made of wood, the fire spread rapidly through the building and burned it to the ground. Joseph, who had been away on business, made his way home as quickly as possible. By the time he reached South Pittsburg the next day, only ashes remained.[44]

Three months after the fire, the company was reborn down the road as the company we now know as Lodge Cast Iron.

Throughout the twentieth century, through creativity and innovation, Lodge Cast Iron survived when most other foundries were forced to shut their doors. Not only has Lodge survived, but it has thrived and offers a broad selection of high-quality cast-iron cookware, which to this day is prized both by the general public and cast-iron collectors.

During the Depression, Lodge kept the doors open and their workers employed by expanding their product line to include novelty items, such as cast-iron garden gnomes and animals.

Following the Depression, as the economy gradually bounced back, Lodge responded to growing business demand by adopting cutting-edge manufacturing techniques. Lodge converted the foundry from a hand-pour operation to an automated molding process. This led to safer and more efficient manufacturing that enabled Lodge to offer a higher-quality, more consistent product at cheaper prices than the competition.

Heading into its second century of business, Lodge continued to innovate. Their president and CEO, Bob Kellermann, led the initiative to preseason each piece of cast-iron cookware in the foundry. In 2002 the process was finalized, and Lodge debuted seasoned cast iron. It was an industry first, which has since become the industry standard.[45]

While domestic competition from foundries such as Wagner and Griswold fell by the wayside, companies such as Le Creuset and Staub from Europe presented a new threat to Lodge Cast Iron. In 2005, Lodge introduced a complementary line of enameled cast iron. This line matches the performance of Le Creuset and Staub enameled cast iron at a much-lower price.

In 2017, Lodge opened a second 127,000-square-foot foundry nicknamed "3rd Street Foundry." This large, state-of-the-art foundry enabled Lodge to increase their manufacturing capacity by 75 percent,[46] making Lodge the largest foundry in the world that manufactures cast-iron cookware.

*Undated photo of the Blacklock Foundry © 2025 Lodge Manufacturing Company*

## Lodge Manufacturing Co.

### Fig 1. Traditional Style "Fluted Cake Pan"

**Width:** 9.7 in. / 24.6 cm
**Height:** 4.2 lbs. / 10.7 cm
**Weight:** 6.6 lbs. / 3.0 kg
**Volume:** 15 cups
**Value:** $100–$150
**Rarity:** ★★

**Description**
Lodge traditional-style "Fluted Tube Pan" with molded, flush surface handles. Earliest versions are marked with an "L" on the underside of one of the handles. Later versions had more-rounded handles, first marked with a single dot, then later with a double dot on the underside of the handles. Probably the most popular cast-iron Bundt pan sold in the US. First introduced in the early 1950s, it was discontinued in 2001. (USA)

Known Collectible Bundt and Gugelhupf Pans 71

## Lodge Manufacturing Company

### Fig 2. Lodge Traditional-Style Legacy Series "Fluted Cake Pan"

**Width:** 10 in. / 25.4 cm
**Height:** 4.25 in. / 10.8 cm
**Weight:** 8.2 lbs. / 3.7 kg
**Volume:** 13 cups
**Value:** $75–$125
**Rarity:** ★

**Description**
The "Lodge Legacy Fluted Cake Pan" is the first of the Lodge the Legacy series, which is a special series of pans based on historical, discontinued Lodge products. They are not exact replicas of old versions but, rather, updated designs with a few small modifications. The Legacy pan has similar molded, flush-surface handles, but they are larger and more squared off. The pan is marked "Lodge" and "1895" on the underside of the handles. The flutes are sharper than the older version. The Legacy was issued in 2018, then rereleased in late 2022. (USA)

## Savery and Company
## Iron Hollow Ware Foundry

The Philadelphia Iron Hollow Ware Foundry, a subsidiary of Savery & Company, was established in 1841 in Philadelphia, Pennsylvania. The foundry operated there until the late nineteenth century and specialized in pots, pans, kettles, and other housewares, in addition to agricultural implements.

## Savery and Company

### Fig 1. "The Washington Cake Pan" Fluted Style Bundt Pan

**Width:** 9.3 in. / 23.6 cm
**Height:** 2.3 in. / 5.8 cm
**Weight:** 4.2 lbs. / 1.9 kg
**Volume:** 6.5 cups
**Value:** $250–$300
**Rarity:** ★★★★★

**Description**
Produced in 1861. Unmarked and double gate marked. Originally known within the collector community as the "Hubcap." The pan was later located in a Savery and Co. catalog dated 1861, listed as a "Washington Cake Pan." (USA)

# Wagner Manufacturing Company

Wagner Manufacturing Company was founded in 1891 by Milton M. and Bernard P. Wagner. However, two more Wagner brothers, Louis and William Wagner, joined the company the following years. Another key player in the foundation of the company was R. Bingham, who previously worked at Marion Stove Company and the Sidney Manufacturing Company. The company was based in Sidney, Ohio.

Although early cookware was simply stamped "Wagner," the term "Wagner Ware" first appeared in the logo in the 1920s.

Wagner was one of the largest American manufacturers of cast-iron products in the twentieth century. The foundry in Sidney operated from 1891 to 1959.

Their product line included skillets, kettles, bean pots, Dutch ovens, roasters, fruit presses, scoops, broilers, griddles, waffle irons, muffin pans, and cornbread pans.

Wagner used different logos and had a range of budget-friendly brands. Wagner labeled their cookware under the following names: Wagner, Wagner Ware Sidney -O-, Wagner Ware, National, Long Life, Magnalite, Wardway, and Ward's Cast Iron. Wagner is best known for the Sidney -O- range of skillets and Dutch ovens.

In the middle of the twentieth century, Wagner began to see a drop in sales, which caused the foundry to struggle financially. This was due to two world wars, the Great Depression, the development of new cookware materials, and the increase of lower-priced imports from Asia. In 1953 the Wagner family sold their interests in the company to the Randell Company.

In 1957, the Randall Company also purchased longtime competitor Griswold from McGraw Edison. The Randall Company was then sold to Textron Corporation in 1959, which was then sold to General Housewares Corporation in 1969. In 1994, all production of Wagner Ware ended.

The Wagner Manufacturing plant in Sidney, Ohio (1913)[47]

# Wagner Manufacturing Company

## Fig 1. "A" Mold–"Prince" Pattern Crown-Style Bundt Pan

**Width:** 8.75 in. / 22.2 cm
**Height:** 4.5 in. / 11.4 cm
**Weight:** 5.9 lbs. / 2.7 kg
**Volume:** 13 cups
**Value:** $1,250–$1,500
**Rarity:** ★★★★★

### Description

Produced in 1915. Made for only one year, making the Wagner "A" extremely rare and sought after by collectors. Sometimes marked "Wagner," "Ware," and "A" on the bottom of the pan. Only known American-made "crown"-style cake pan. Modeled after the "Royal Prince" from Gottbill Eisenwerk in Germany. Available in both cast iron and aluminum. (USA)

# Wagner Manufacturing Company

Wagner Manufacturing Company was founded in 1891 by Milton M. and Bernard P. Wagner. However, two more Wagner brothers, Louis and William Wagner, joined the company the following years. Another key player in the foundation of the company was R. Bingham, who previously worked at Marion Stove Company and the Sidney Manufacturing Company. The company was based in Sidney, Ohio.

Although early cookware was simply stamped "Wagner," the term "Wagner Ware" first appeared in the logo in the 1920s.

Wagner was one of the largest American manufacturers of cast-iron products in the twentieth century. The foundry in Sidney operated from 1891 to 1959.

Their product line included skillets, kettles, bean pots, Dutch ovens, roasters, fruit presses, scoops, broilers, griddles, waffle irons, muffin pans, and cornbread pans.

Wagner used different logos and had a range of budget-friendly brands. Wagner labeled their cookware under the following names: Wagner, Wagner Ware Sidney -O-, Wagner Ware, National, Long Life, Magnalite, Wardway, and Ward's Cast Iron. Wagner is best known for the Sidney -O- range of skillets and Dutch ovens.

In the middle of the twentieth century, Wagner began to see a drop in sales, which caused the foundry to struggle financially. This was due to two world wars, the Great Depression, the development of new cookware materials, and the increase of lower-priced imports from Asia. In 1953 the Wagner family sold their interests in the company to the Randell Company.

In 1957, the Randall Company also purchased longtime competitor Griswold from McGraw Edison. The Randall Company was then sold to Textron Corporation in 1959, which was then sold to General Housewares Corporation in 1969. In 1994, all production of Wagner Ware ended.

The Wagner Manufacturing plant in Sidney, Ohio (1913)[47]

# Wagner Manufacturing Company

## Fig 1. "A" Mold—"Prince" Pattern Crown-Style Bundt Pan

**Width:** 8.75 in. / 22.2 cm
**Height:** 4.5 in. / 11.4 cm
**Weight:** 5.9 lbs. / 2.7 kg
**Volume:** 13 cups
**Value:** $1,250–$1,500
**Rarity:** ★★★★★

**Description**
Produced in 1915. Made for only one year, making the Wagner "A" extremely rare and sought after by collectors. Sometimes marked "Wagner," "Ware," and "A" on the bottom of the pan. Only known American-made "crown"-style cake pan. Modeled after the "Royal Prince" from Gottbill Eisenwerk in Germany. Available in both cast iron and aluminum. (USA)

# Wagner Manufacturing Company

## How to Distinguish a Wagner "A" from a "Royal Prince"

Among collectors there has been some confusion and difficulty distinguishing a Wagner "A" mold from a German "Royal Prince" by Gottbill sel Erben Eisenwerk. Not only were the two pans cast in two different countries (United States and Germany), but the value of the Wagner "A" ($650–$750) is about five times more than the value of the "Royal Prince" ($125–$150). At first glance the two pans look identical, but on closer inspection there are some subtle differences that enable collectors to distinguish between the two pans.

**Wagner "A" mold (USA)**        **Gottbill Royal Prince (Germany)**

One of the easiest ways to tell the two pans apart is to compare the markings on both pans. A marked Wagner "A" is marked "Wagner Ware" on the bottom of the pan, and a marked "Royal Prince" contains the Gottbill Eisenwerk mark and the number "22" on the base of the pan.

**Wagner "A" mold (USA)**

*Image courtesy of Chris Kendall*

**Gottbill Royal Prince (Germany)**

**76** COLLECTIBLE CAST IRON

**Wagner "A" mold (USA)**

**Gottbill Royal Prince (Germany)**

If unmarked, the easiest way to tell the difference between the two pans is to check the tubes of each pan. The tube on the Gottbill "Royal Prince" has a smooth tip that is longer than that of the Wagner "A" Bundt.

The next step is to check for sprue or gate marks. If there are gate marks on the bottom of the pan, it is likely an unmarked "Royal Prince" from Gottbill sel Erben Eisenwerk. If the pan has no gate marks or sprue marks, but instead has grind marks on the outside rim of the pan, this shows that the pan is side gated and is most likely a Wagner "A" mold.

If the pan is sprue marked, this means that the pan is likely a recast of either the Wagner or the Gottbill pan.

Lastly, the handles on the Wagner "A" mold (left) are smaller and have a rougher cast than on the larger, and more refined handles of the "Gottbill Royal Prince (right).

**Wagner "A" mold (side gated)**

**Gottbill Royal Prince (gate marked)**

Known Collectible Bundt and Gugelhupf Pans 77

# Wagner Manufacturing Company

## Fig 2. "B" Mold—Traditional-Style Bundt Pan

**Width:** 10.0 in. / 25.5 cm
**Height:** 4.4 in. / 11.1 cm
**Weight:** 7.8 lbs. / 3.56 kg
**Volume:** 17 cups
**Value:** $225–$500
**Rarity:** ★★

### Description

Ca. 1914. Traditional-style Bundt. Easily identifiable small, reinforced tab handles. (USA) Four variations exist:
- unmarked
- marked "Wagner Ware"
- marked "Wagner Ware" and "B" for the pattern number
- marked "Wagner Ware" and "B" for the pattern number "1310" (pictured)

# Węgierska Górka Eisenwerk
## (Węgierska Górka, Poland)

In 1838, Adam Wielopolski founded an ironworks in Węgierska Górka, Poland. The first kiln was launched in 1840. The ore was mined in the villages of Kamesznica, Ujsół, Milówka, Jeleśnia, and Rychwałd in Poland. In July 1844, Archduke Charles Louis Habsburg expanded the steelworks and equipped it with four hammers.

A second blast furnace was launched in December 1852. By this time the foundry was producing hearth doors, grates, channel gratings, machine castings, hydrants, linen boilers, pots, and saucepans. The goods were sold in the countries of the Austro-Hungarian monarchy. Between 1841 and 1870, production increased eight times.

After 1918, the steelworks were transformed into a public company, seeing investment from Czech and French capital. After modernization, the steelworks were transformed into the Metalpol Węgierska Górka foundry and have been owned since 2000 by the French CF2M Foundry and Metallurgy Group.[48]

Mark displaying the crown of the Habsburg coat of arms, the Maltese cross, and the abbreviation "TSN" for "Teschen" which is the region in Poland.

The town of Węgierska Górka is historically significant, because from September 1 to 3, 1939, it was invaded by the German Wehrmacht, which is considered the beginning of World War II.

Dolman pattern pan from Węgierska Górka Eisenwerk displaying their "Teschen" mark.

## Węgierska Górka Eisenwerk

### Fig 1. "Dolman" Pattern Crown Style Cake Pan—Marked "Teschen"

**Width:** 9.8 in. / 25 cm
**Height:** 4.1 in. / 10.3 cm
**Weight:** 6.8 lbs. / 3.1 kg
**Volume:** 13 cups
**Value:** $250–$300
**Rarity:** ★★★★★

**Description**

Crown-style pan in the "Dolman" pattern. Extremely rare. Can be found in plain cast iron, white enamel interior, or enameled interior and exterior. The pictured pan is a survivor in as-found condition. It is cracked and has one handle missing and displays the "Teschen" mark and the number "2," which is assumed to be the pattern number for the pan. There are several examples of cast-iron cookware that contain the "TSN" or "Teschen" mark (or both). (Poland)

# Železárny a Smaltovny Bartelmus a.s. (Pilsen, Czech Republic)

Eduard Bartelmus, a Czech chemist and inventor of German nationality, became the pioneer of enameled cast iron in the early 1830s, when he made the discovery of environmentally healthful enamel that did not release any poisonous heavy metals. This made it ideal for the production of enameled metal kitchenware.

In 1832, he opened the first enamelware factory in Brno, in what is now known as the Czech Republic. In 1868, he sold his factory and built a larger, more modern enameling factory and foundry in Pilsen, known as Železárny a Smaltovny Bartelmus a.s. in 1870 (Bartelmus Enamel and Ironworks).

The Bartelmus factory produced all kinds of enameled baking pans, saucepans, pots, and lids, as well as teapots and spoons. His enamelware came in many colors, but most commonly in blue. He succeeded in demonstrating on a large scale the benefits of enameled cookware over the traditional kitchenware available at the time.

In addition to the cast-iron items that were produced in the Bartelmus factory, other cast-iron cookware was also sourced from other foundries. One such foundry partner was "Komárovské železárny" (Komárov Ironworks), later known as Buzuluk a.s. Komárov supplied Bartelmus with everything from cast-iron roasters and pots to shallow cake forms and "babovku" (Bundt) pans.

Most of the cast-iron enamelware produced by Bartelmus is marked with the word "Pilsen" and is frequently followed by a "18*70" and a pattern number. However, none of the shallow cake forms or "babovku" pans are known to be marked. It is thought that this is because the raw cast-iron cake pans were produced by Komárov Ironworks and only enameled by Bartelmus.

By 1896 the Bartelmus factory had grown to five hundred employees and operated until being nationalized by the Communist Party in Czechoslovakia in February 1948.

# Železárny a Smaltovny Bartelmus a.s.

## Figs. 1-4. Bartelmus "Babovku" Enamelware

**Fig 1. Bartelmus "Big Bake Mold"**

**Width:** 10.25 in. / 26 cm
**Height:** Height: 4.33 in. / 11 cm
**Weight:** 6.4 lbs. / 2.9 kg
**Volume:** 14 cups
**Value:** $100–$150
**Rarity:** ★★

**Fig 2. Bartelmus "Duchess"**

**Width:** 10.2 in. / 25 9 cm
**Height:** 3.5 in. / 8.9 cm
**Weight:** 6.6 lbs. / 3 kg
**Volume:** 9 cups
**Value:** $250–$350
**Rarity:** ★★★

**Fig 3. Bartelmus "Dolman"**

**Width:** 9.8 in. / 25 cm
**Height:** 4.1 in. / 10.3 cm
**Weight:** 6.8 lbs. / 3.1 kg
**Volume:** 13 cups
**Value:** $100–$150
**Rarity:** ★★★

**Fig 4. Bartelmus "Lady"**

**Width:** 8.8 in. / 22.3 cm
**Height:** 4.4 in. / 11.2 cm
**Weight:** 5.5 lbs. / 2.45 kg
**Volume:** 13 cups
**Value:** $100–$150
**Rarity:** ★★★

# Unknown Traditional-Style Bundt and Gugelhupf Pans

# Unknown Traditional-Style Cake Pans

## Fig 1. The "Emperor"

**Width:** 12.2 in. / 31.0 cm
**Height:** 4.9 in. / 12.5 cm
**Weight:** 8.4 lbs. / 3.8 kg
**Volume:** 31 cups
**Value:** $200–$225
**Rarity:** ★★★

**Description**
Traditional-style gugelhupf. A diameter of 31 cm and a 31-cup volume make this the largest of the gugelhupf pans. (Germany)

# Unknown Traditional-Style Cake Pans

## Fig 2. The "Kingdom"

**Width:** 11.5 in. / 29.2 cm
**Height:** 5.5 in. / 14.0 cm
**Weight:** 10.6 lbs. / 4.8 kg
**Volume:** 24 cups
**Value:** $175–$250
**Rarity:** ★★★

**Description**

Large, traditional-style gugelhupf mounted on a plane base. Can be gate marked or sprue marked. The pictured example displays four monster sprue marks that are so big that they double as feet for the pan. Unrestored pan in as-found condition. (Germany)

## Unknown Traditional-Style Cake Pans

### Fig 3. The "Millennial"

**Width:** 10.75 in. / 27.5 cm
**Height:** 4.92 in. / 12.5 cm
**Weight:** 8.6 lbs. / 3.9 kg
**Volume:** 15 cups
**Value:** $250–$300
**Rarity:** ★★★★

**Description**
Traditional-style mold with a "helper" ring and molded handles. The pictured example displays six prominent sprue marks on the bottom of the pan. Similar design as the "Kingdom," though smaller. (Germany)

*Primary photo courtesy of Marc Wissen*

# Unknown Traditional Style Cake Pans

## Fig 4. Oval Shaped Traditional Style Cake Pan

**Width:** 11.5 × 9.75 in. / 29.2 × 24.8 cm
**Height:** 3 1/2 in. / 8.9 cm
**Weight:** 8.3 lbs. / 3.8 kg
**Volume:** 12 cups
**Value:** $350–$400
**Rarity:** ★★★★★

**Description**
Traditional-style Bundt pan with an oval shape. Has sprue marks and comes with either squared-off or rounded, welded-on handles. More commonly found in aluminum, but a few cast-iron versions can be found. (Germany)

*Images courtesy of Rhonda Owen*

# Unknown Traditional-Style Cake Pans

## Fig 5. The "Poser"

**Width:** 9.7 in. / 24.6 cm
**Height:** 4.6 in. / 11.6 cm
**Weight:** 7.7 lbs. / 3.5 kg
**Volume:** 10 cups
**Value:** $175–$200
**Rarity:** ★★★

**Description**
Plain and basic gugelhupf with slight traditional-style features. Smooth inner tube with molded handles. (Germany)

## Unknown Traditional-Style Cake Pans

### Fig 6. Traditional Style Bundt Pan with Bailed Handle

**Width:** 10.3 in. / 26.2 cm
**Height:** 4.8 in. / 12.1 cm
**Weight:** 8.4 lbs. / 3.8 kg
**Volume:** 12 cups
**Value:** $150–$250
**Rarity:** ★★★★

**Description**
Unmarked, traditional-style Bundt pan with a bailed handle. Sprue marked. Rare to find with the bailed handle still attached. Only known American Bundt pan, other than the Griswold 965 and the (Griswold-produced) Frank Hay & Sons Bundt pan with a bail handle. (USA)

## Unknown Traditional-Style Cake Pans

### Fig 7. Traditional Style Bundt Pan—XL Un-Reinforced Handles

   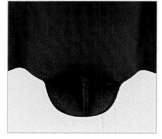

**Width:** 10.0 in. / 25.4 cm
**Height:** 4.5 in. / 11.4 cm
**Weight:** 9.7 lbs. / 4.4 kg
**Volume:** 17 cups
**Value:** $75–$125
**Rarity:** ★★

**Description**
Traditional-style Bundt pans with extra-large, tab-style handles. Double gate marked. Commonly mistaken for the Wagner "B" mold. Wagner "Bs" have smaller, reinforced handles and a superior cast and never had gate marks. (USA)

## Unknown Traditional-Style Cake Pans

### Fig 8. Traditional Style Bundt Pan—XL Reinforced Handles (I)

  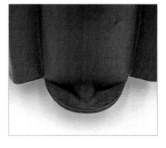 

**Width:** 9.5 in. / 2.41 cm
**Height:** 4.25 in. / 10.8 cm
**Weight:** 7.1 lbs. / 3.2 kg
**Volume:** 14 cups
**Value:** $75–$125
**Rarity:** ★★

**Description**
Traditional-style Bundt pan with extra-large, tab-style reinforced handles. In this version the handle has a reinforcement, and the handle thickness is relatively thin. Sprue marked. Commonly mistaken for the Wagner "B" mold. Wagner "Bs" have smaller, reinforced handles and a superior cast and never had sprue marks. (USA)

# Unknown Traditional-Style Cake Pans

## Fig 9. Traditional Style Bundt Pan—XL Reinforced Handles (II)

**Width:** 10.0 in. / 25.4 cm
**Height:** 4.5 in. / 11.4 cm
**Weight:** 9.1 lbs. / 4.1 kg
**Volume:** 15 cups
**Value:** $75–$125
**Rarity:** ★★

**Description**

Traditional-style Bundt pan with extra-large, tab-style reinforced handles. In this version the handles are slightly pointed and thicker. Double gate marked. Commonly mistaken for the Wagner "B" mold. Wagner "Bs" have smaller, thinner, reinforced handles and a superior cast and never had sprue or gate marks. One example has an "E.G.E." mark on the underside of the handle. (USA)

## Unknown Traditional-Style Cake Pans

### Fig 10. Traditional Style Bundt Pan with "Pierced Ear" Tab Handles

**Width:** 10.2 in. / 25.9 cm
**Height:** 4.5 in. / 11.5 cm
**Weight:** 8.3 lbs. / 3.75 kg
**Volume:** 16 cups
**Value:** $75–$125
**Rarity:** ★★★

**Description**
American traditional-style pan with large tab handles. Both handles have beveled "pierced ear" looking holes. (USA)

94 COLLECTIBLE CAST IRON

## Unknown Traditional-Style Cake Pans

### Fig 11. Traditional Style Bundt Pan with "Bottle Opener" Handles

**Width:** 9.5 in. / 24.2 cm
**Height:** 4.45 in. / 11.3 cm
**Weight:** 8.8 lbs. / 4.0 kg
**Volume:** 16 cups
**Value:** $75–$125
**Rarity:** ★★

**Description**
Traditional-style design with sprue marks and "bottle opener"-looking tabbed handles. Sprue marked. (USA)

# Unknown Traditional-Style Cake Pans

## Fig 12. Traditional Style Bundt Pan with "Propeller" Handles (I)

**Width:** 10.4 in. / 26.4 cm
**Height:** 8.3 in. / 21.1 cm
**Weight:** 7.1 lbs. / 3.2 kg
**Volume:** 14 cups
**Value:** $100–$150
**Rarity:** ★★★

**Description**

Traditional-style gugelhupf pan. Large, distinct sprue marks. Flat, long "propeller" tab handles make this pan easy to spot. Sometimes customized with the buyer's initials on the side of the pan. (Germany)

## Unknown Traditional-Style Cake Pans

### Fig 13. Traditional Style Bundt Pan with "Propeller" Handles (II)

   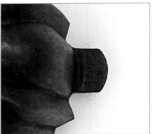

**Width:** 10.3 in. / 26.2 cm
**Height:** 4.5 in. / 11.4 cm
**Weight:** 7.5 lbs. / 3.4 kg
**Volume:** 14 cups
**Value:** $100–$150
**Rarity:** ★★★★

**Description**
Traditional-style gugelhupf pan. Flat, long "propeller" tab handles that are slightly rounded. Four pronounced sprue marks and handle design distinguish this from the much more common "Propeller I" gugelhupf. (Germany)

# Unknown Traditional-Style Cake Pans

## Fig 14. Traditional Style Bundt Pan with Ring Handles

**Width:** 10.6 in. / 26.9 cm
**Height:** 5.0 in. / 12.8 cm
**Weight:** 7.1 lbs. / 3.2 kg
**Volume:** 14 cups
**Value:** $100–$150
**Rarity:** ★★★★

**Description**

Traditional-style gugelhupf pan with pronounced sprue marks. Has vertical tab handles with holes for anchoring ring handles. Rare example with both rings still attached. Pans with vertical handles can contain either rings (pictured) or bailed handles. Bundts with rings are most commonly from Germany, while the bail-handled version (except for the German Petromax) are thought to be from the US. (USA)

## Unknown Traditional-Style Cake Pans

### Fig 15. Traditional-style Bundt with beveled handles

**Width:** 10.25 in. / 26 cm
**Height:** 4.75 in. / 12.1 cm
**Weight:** 8.9 lbs. / 4.0 kg
**Volume:** 19 cups
**Value:** $100–$150
**Rarity:** ★ ★ ★ ★

**Description**
Traditional-style gugelhupf pan with pronounced, double-sprue-marked bottom. Has unique beveled handles that are welded onto the pan. (Germany)

# Unknown Crown-Style Bundt and Gugelhupf Pans

## Unknown Crown-Style Pans

### Fig 1. The "Dominion"

**Width:** 10.4 in. / 26.5 cm
**Height:** 4.1 in. / 10.5 cm
**Weight:** 5.7 lbs. / 2.6 kg
**Volume:** 11 cups
**Value:** $250–$350
**Rarity:** ★★★

**Description**

Crown-style pan with four stacked arches atop an elevated, ornate base. Not to be confused with the "Duchess," which has five arches on a low, ornate base. Sprue marked. Often found with an enameled interior and exterior. Frequently marked with an "8" but occasionally can be found with a "5" or a "3" mark. These marks are thought to identify the mold used in the cast. A few examples are also marked with an "88," which is presumed to be an unknown foundry mark. The "88" mark has also been found on a "Monarch," a "Dominion," and a traditional-style gugelhupf pan. A variant of the regular "Dominion" exists with a slightly larger diameter and a much-taller base. Only one example is known to exist. (Czech Republic)

# Unknown Crown-Style Pans

## Fig 2. The "Excelsior" (Triple Crown Series)

**Width:** 12.0 in. / 30.6 cm
**Height:** 4.6 in. / 11.6 cm
**Weight:** 10.8 lbs. / 4.9 kg
**Volume:** 25 cups
**Value:** $250–$400
**Rarity:** ★★★★

**Description**
Double-fluted design. Single gate mark and comes with or without handles. Often found with an enameled interior. Marked with a "10." Seldom seen until recently. Many known examples have been tracked back to France. (France)

102  COLLECTIBLE CAST IRON

# Unknown Crown-Style Pans

## Fig 3. The "Grand Duke" (Triple Crown Series)

**Width:** 10.4 in. / 26.4 cm
**Height:** 4.2 in. / 10.6 cm
**Weight:** 6.3 lbs. / 2.83 kg
**Volume:** 16 cups
**Value:** $200–$275
**Rarity:** ★★★★

**Description**
Crown-style pan with rows of "Vs" on top of an ornate base. Often found with enameled interior. One example is marked with a "WR." Part of the "Triple Crown" series. (Germany)

Unknown Crown-Style Bundt and Gugelhupf Pans 103

# Unknown Crown-Style Pans

## Fig 4. The "King" (Triple Crown Series)

**Width:** 10.5 in. / 26.7 cm
**Height:** 4.4 in. / 11.1 cm
**Weight:** 6.8 lbs. / 3.128 kg
**Volume:** 17 cups
**Value:** $250–$350
**Rarity:** ★★★

**Description**
Large, crown-style pan with welded-on handles. Very hard to obtain in a noncracked condition. Part of the "Triple Crown" series. (Germany)

## Unknown Crown-Style Pans

### Fig 5. The "Monarch" (Triple Crown Series)

**Width:** 8.9 in. / 22.5 cm
**Height:** 3.8 in. / 9.6 cm
**Weight:** 6 lbs. / 2.7 kg
**Volume:** 11 cups
**Value:** $150–$200
**Rarity:** ★★★

**Description**
Crown-style pan with molded handles. Has "V" patterns atop an ornate base. A few display an "88." It is possibly an unknown foundry mark, since the "88" mark has also been found on "Dominion"-patterned pans, as well as on a traditional-style gugelhupf pan. Part of the "Triple Crown" series. (Czech Republic / Germany)

# Unknown Crown-Style Pans

## Fig 6. The "Prince" (Triple Crown Series)

**Width:** 8.3 in. / 21.0 cm
**Height:** 3.4 in / 8.7 cm
**Weight:** 3.5 lbs. / 1.60 kg
**Volume:** 8 cups
**Value:** $200–$275
**Rarity:** ★★★

**Description**
Smaller crown-style pan, double gate marked with welded-on handles. About half the size of the Triple Crown "King." Part of the "Triple Crown" series. (Germany)

## Unknown Crown-Style Pans

### Fig 7. The "Princess" (Triple Crown Series)

**Width:** 9.6 in. / 24.3 cm
**Height:** 4.0 in. / 10.2
**Weight:** 7.5 lbs. / 3.4 kg
**Volume:** 10 cups
**Value:** $1,250–$1,500
**Rarity:** ★★★★★

**Description**

Crown-style pan. The most collectible of all Bundt pans—only three are known to exist. One is marked with a "5" and an "R." Part of the "Triple Crown" series. (France/Germany)

*Images courtesy of Rhonda Owen*

# Unknown Crown-Style Pans

## The "Princess"

Of the known "Princess" gugelhupfs, there are two variations:

**Variation 1**

Rounded, welded-on handles. Bubbles have two low bases. Bubbles descend into the tube. Marked with a "5" and an "R."
*Image courtesy of Marc Wissen*

**Variation 2**

Square, welded-on handles. Bubbles have two high bases. Bubbles separate from the tube.

Eight-sided tube. Bubbles flow into the tube. *Image courtesy of Marc Wissen*

Smooth tube. Bubbles separate from the tube.
*Image courtesy of Rhonda Owen*

# Unknown Crown-Style Pans

## The "Princess," "Napfkuchen Form als Hut" (Cake Mold as a Hat)

The image on this vintage postcard of a lady wearing a gugelhupf pan on her head is well known in the Bundt pan collector community. This image is significant because, until 2020, it was the only image of the "Princess" gugelhupf known to exist. But recently, three examples of the "Princess" gugelhupf have surfaced. With only three known to exist at this time, the "Princess" is the most collectible and desirable of all German gugelhupfs.

Interestingly, the pan in the postcard is slightly different from known "Princess" pans that have so far been discovered. Most notably, the pan in the postcard has no handles, while the three known examples of the "Princess" have handles.

Also, the upper top / bubbletop of the pan in the postcard more closely resembles the top of the first pan (variation #1).

The woman in this postcard is a bit of a mystery. Postcard collectors have yet to find out any history on her . . . even her name. She was one of the more prolific models appearing on German postcards in the decade following the turn of the century.

As a child model, she appeared in many "family at home and at play" images in the early 1900s. As a young woman, ca. 1907–12, she modeled hats—big ones, small ones, fancy ones, plain ones, and, apparently, even a cast-iron one. This postcard was from a popular series produced in 1910 titled "Non plus ultra," a Latin phrase meaning "Nothing Can Top This."[49]

**Postcard**

**Variation 1**

**Variation 2**

## Unknown Crown-Style Pans

### Fig 8. The "Queen" (Triple Crown Series)

**Width:** 10.6 in. / 27 cm
**Height:** 4.3 in. / 11 cm
**Weight:** 9.7 lbs. / 4.40 kg
**Volume:** 16 cups
**Value:** $250–$350
**Rarity:** ★★★★

**Description**
Crown-style pan with a twisted braid on top, sitting on an ornate base. Smooth tube. Usually found with a white or blue enameled interior. Sprue marks. Part of the "Triple Crown" series. (Germany)

# Unknown Crown-Style Pans

## Fig 9. The "Queen"

**Width:** 10.2 in. / 26 cm
**Height:** 5.0 in. / 12.7 cm
**Weight:** 7.7 lbs. / 3.50 kg
**Volume:** 21 cups
**Value:** $250–$350
**Rarity:** ★★★

**Description**

Queen-style crown gugelhupf with double gate marks and molded handles. Sometimes marked with a "26." Most likely an unmarked version or recast of the "Queen" from the Gottbill sel. Erben Eisenwerk, depending on the pan. Sentimental favorite among many bakers in the US. Unrestored pan in as-found condition. (German)

Unknown Crown-Style Bundt and Gugelhupf Pans  111

# Unknown Crown-Style Pans

## Fig 10. The "Wissen"

**Width:** Unknown
**Height:** Unknown
**Weight:** Unknown
**Volume:** 6 cups
**Value:** $250–$300
**Rarity:** ★★★★★

**Description**

Crown-style pan. Gate marked on an elevated, ornate base. Found with a blue-enameled exterior and a white-enameled interior, which was later removed. Named after a popular German dealer who sells to the American collector community. (Germany)

*Images courtesy of Marc Wissen*

# Unknown Crown-Style Pans

## Fig 11. Small Crown Style Pan

**Width:** 7.2 in. / 18.2 cm
**Height:** 3.7 in. / 9.5 cm
**Weight:** 2.65 lbs. / 1.2 kg
**Volume:** 4 cups
**Value:** $250–$300
**Rarity:** ★★★★★

**Description**

Crown-style design, sitting on a plain base with welded-on handles. Sprue marked with an enamel interior. Marked with a number "4." Extremely rare. (Germany)

# Unknown Fluted-Style Bundt and Gugelhupf Pans

## Unknown Fluted-Style Pans

### Fig 1. "Adelaide" Fluted Style Pan (Triple Crown Series)

**Width:** 5.9 in. / 15 cm
**Height:** 2.6 in. / 7.5 cm
**Weight:** 2.8 lbs. / 1.25 kg
**Volume:** 2 cups
**Value:** $350–$450
**Rarity:** ★★★★

**Description**
Small, fluted-style cake pan on an ornate base. Comes with and without handles. Part of the "Triple Crown" series. (Germany)

# Unknown Fluted-Style Pans

## Fig 2. "Aristocracy"

**Width:** 9.5 in. / 24 cm
**Height:** 4.0 in. / 10.2 cm
**Weight:** Unknown
**Volume:** 18 cups
**Value:** $250–$350
**Rarity:** ★★★★★

**Description**

Fluted-style cake pan with welded-on handles. Similar to the Aristocrat but has twenty-four alternating rounded and pointed flutes and a smooth tube. Extremely rare. (German)

*Images courtesy of Marc Wisson and Hoger Bolgin*

## Unknown Fluted-Style Pans

### Fig 3. The "Aristocrat"

**Width:** 10.2 in. / 26 cm
**Height:** 4.3 in. / 11.0 cm
**Weight:** 6.1 lbs. / 2.75 kg
**Volume:** 17 cups
**Value:** $125–$175
**Rarity:** ★★★

**Description**
Fluted-style cake pan with tight ruffles makes this reminiscent of the traditional-style gugelhupf. (Germany / Czech Republic)

Unknown Fluted-Style Bundt and Gugelhupf Pans  117

## Unknown Fluted-Style Pans

### Fig 4. The "Carnival"

**Width:** 10.6 in. / 27 cm
**Height:** 4.7 in. / 12 cm
**Weight:** 7.8 lbs. / 3.465 kg
**Volume:** 19 cups
**Value:** $175–$250
**Rarity:** ★★★★

**Description**
Fluted-style cake pan with molded handles. Sharp, uniform flutes with a unique, smooth inner tube design. Two very pronounced gate marks.

## Unknown Fluted-Style Pans

### Fig 5. The "Cathedral"

**Width:** 11.7 in. / 29.7 cm
**Height:** 5.2 in. / 13.3 cm
**Weight:** 12.8 lbs. / 5.8 kg
**Volume:** 27 cups
**Value:** $1,250–$2,500
**Rarity:** ★★★★★

**Description**
Majestic fluted-style pan with no handles. Comes with sprue marks or gate marks. One of the largest gugelhupf pans available. Has cathedral-type arches. One of the most collectible and desirable of all gugelhupf pans. (Germany)

Unknown Fluted-Style Bundt and Gugelhupf Pans 119

# Unknown Fluted-Style Pans

## Fig 6. The "Pauper"

   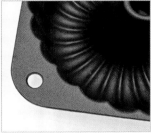

**Width:** 11.4 in. / 23.0 cm
**Height:** 3.5 in. / 8.9 cm
**Weight:** 9.0 lbs. / 4.1 kg
**Volume:** 12 cups
**Value:** $150–$200
**Rarity:** ★★

**Description**
Simple, fluted design. Sits on a flat, square base with a hole for hanging. (Germany)

# Unknown Fluted-Style Pans

## Fig 7. The "Reichsritter," Marked "ERM"

**Width:** 8.8 in. / 22.4 cm
**Height:** 4.4 in. / 11.1 cm
**Weight:** 7.9 lbs. / 3.16 kg
**Volume:** 10 cups
**Value:** $350–$400
**Rarity:** ★★★★

**Description**

"Reichsritter" means "imperial knight" in German. Fluted-style gugelhupf pan. Very smooth casting with a closed tube. One tab marked with "550," one with "ERM" (unknown) maker's mark. (Germany)

## Unknown Fluted-Style Pans

### Fig. 9. Small Fluted-Style Bundt Pan

**Width:** 5.9 in. / 15.0 cm
**Height:** 3.0 in. / 7.6 cm
**Weight:** 2.6 lbs. / 1.2 kg
**Volume:** 2 cups
**Value:** $500–$750
**Rarity:** ★★★★★

**Description**
Unknown fluted swirl pan on a plain base. Can be found with or without handles. Gate marked on the bottom. Reminiscent of the "Adelaide" without the swirls or the ornate base. Extremely rare and sought after. (Germany)

# Unknown
# Swirl-Style Bundt
# and Gugelhupf Pans

# Unknown Swirl-Style Pans

## Fig 1. The "Cyclone"

**Width:** 11.2 in. / 28.5 cm
**Height:** 5.1 in. / 12.9 cm
**Weight:** 9.5 lbs. / 4.27 kg
**Volume:** 24 cups
**Value:** $175–$250
**Rarity:** ★★★★★

**Description**
Swirl-style gugelhupf. Double gate marked with molded handles and a smooth tube. Likely an unmarked version of the cyclone-style pan listed in a 1933 Gottbill catalog (fig. 26). (German)

# Unknown Swirl-Style Pans

## Fig 2. The "Cyclone Jr."

**Width:** 10.3 in. / 26 cm
**Height:** 5.6 in. / 14.1 cm
**Weight:** 7.5 lbs. / 3.35 kg
**Volume:** 14 cups
**Value:** $250–$300
**Rarity:** ★★★★

**Description**
Similar to the "Cyclone" but about half the size, with a tapered swirl pattern. Smooth tube on the inside with double gate marks. Sometimes found with an enameled exterior. (Germany)

## Unknown Swirl-Style Pans

### Fig 3. The "Duchess Wolfe"

**Width:** 8.3 in. / 21 cm
**Height:** 4.7 in. / 12 cm
**Weight:** 4.2 lbs. / 1.9 kg
**Volume:** 8 cups

**Width:** 9.6 in. / 24.3 cm
**Height:** 4.6 in. / 11.7 cm
**Weight:** 7.9 lbs. / 3.6 kg
**Volume:** 15 cups

**Width:** 10.8 in. / 27.5 cm
**Height:** 5.5 in. / 14 cm
**Weight:** 11 lbs. / 5 kg
**Volume:** 22 cups

**Value:** $150–$225
**Rarity:** ★★★

**Description**

Comes in three sizes. Swirl-style pan that sits atop a flat base. Comes with either sprue or gate marks. Can have an enameled interior. Sometimes marked with a "3." Often confused with the "Hurricane," but the swirls go straight up the tube on the Duchess Wolfe and they swirl up the tube in the "Hurricane." (Germany)

## Unknown Swirl-Style Pans

### Fig 4. "Edeltraud"

**Width:** 7.5 in. / 19 cm
**Height:** 3.9 in. / 10 cm
**Weight:** 3.3 lbs. / 1.5 kg
**Volume:** 7 cups
**Value:** $250–$325
**Rarity:** ★★★★

**Description**
"Edeltraud" translates to "noble strength." A smaller swirl-style pan with plane handles, mounted atop an ornate base. Often found with enamel interior and exterior. (Czech Republic)

## Unknown Swirl-Style Pans

### Fig 5. The "Gentleman"

**Width:** 10.4 in. / 26.4 cm
**Height:** 4.2 in. / 10.7 cm
**Weight:** 7.3 lbs. / 3.3 kg
**Volume:** 14 cups
**Value:** $175–$250
**Rarity:** ★ ★ ★

**Description**

Swirl-style pan with plain handles mounted atop an ornate base. Sometimes found enameled on both the inside and the outside. Comes with and without handles. Thought to be from Germany, but several have been found in France and the Czech Republic. A variation can be found with a solid tube and a ring welded to the outside. (Germany, France, Czech Republic)

# Unknown Swirl-Style Pans

## Fig 6. The "Hurricane"

**Width:** 8.6 in. / 21.8 cm
**Height:** 5.0 in. / 12.7 cm
**Weight:** 4.4 lbs. / 2.0 kg
**Volume:** 8 cups

**Width:** 9.9 in. / 25.1 cm
**Height:** 3.8 in. / 9.7 cm
**Weight:** 6.5 lbs. / 2.9 kg
**Volume:** 12 cups

**Width:** 11.5 in. / 29.2 cm
**Height:** 3.1 in. / 7.9 cm
**Weight:** 9.1 lbs. / 4.1 kg
**Volume:** 24 cups

**Value:** $150–$200
**Rarity:** ★ ★ ★

**Description**
Double gate marked with a spiral tube. Comes in three sizes, with or without handles. Possibly unmarked versions of the "Hurricane" from Gottbill Eisenwerk. Sometimes confused with the "Duchess Wolfe," but the swirls spiral up the tube on the Hurricane and they go straight up the tube on the Duchess Wolfe. (Germany)

# Unknown Swirl-Style Pans

## How to Distinguish a "Hurricane" from a "Duchess Wolfe"

Both pans are swirl pans. Both can be found with or without handles. Both sit on a flat base and come in three sizes. How do you tell them apart? There are two easy ways to tell.

The swirls on the Hurricane have a smooth, consistent curve to them. On the Duchess Wolfe, the swirls have a sharper, less uniform curve to them.

The swirls on the tube on the Hurricane swirl up the tube. On the Duchess Wolfe, the swirls go straight up the tube, and the tube has a larger diameter.

**Hurricane**

**Duchess Wolfe**

**Hurricane**

**Duchess Wolfe**

## Unknown Swirl-Style Pans

### Fig 7. The "Twister I"

**Width:** 11.6 in. / 29.4 cm
**Height:** 4.4 in. / 11.2 cm
**Weight:** 8.2 lbs. / 3.65 kg
**Volume:** 20 cups
**Value:** Small $250–$300 / Large $175–$250
**Rarity:** ★★★

**Description**

Classic, swirl-style pan. Usually has double gate marks or sprue marks with welded-on, ring-style handles. Sometimes found with an enamel interior. An extremely rare, smaller version of the "Twister I" also exists. (Germany)

# Unknown Swirl-Style Pans

## Fig 8. The "Twister II"

   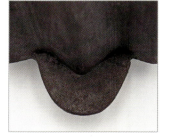

**Width:** 9.8 in. / 24.8 cm
**Height:** 3.75 in. / 9.5 cm
**Weight:** 5.5 lbs. / 2.5 kg
**Volume:** 12 cups
**Value:** $250–$300

**Width:** 11.5 in. / 29.2 cm
**Height:** 4.75 in. / 12.0 cm
**Weight:** 7.8 lbs. / 3.5 kg
**Volume:** 21 cups
**Value:** $150–$250

**Description**

Comes in two sizes. A swirl-style "Twister" gugelhupf with sprue marked bottom and molded, tab-style handles. Often found with customized initials of the purchaser on the handles. A smaller version of the "Twister II" also exists but is extremely rare. (Germany)

Unknown Swirl-Style Bundt and Gugelhupf Pans   133

# Unknown Swirl-Style Pans

### Fig 9. "Vater Brinkhaus"

**Width:** 27 cm
**Height:** 10.5 cm
**Weight:** 2.8 kg
**Volume:** 12 cups
**Value:** $275–$350
**Rarity:** ★★★

**Description**

"Vater Brinkhaus" translates to "Father Brinkhaus." This swirl-style pan has swirls mounted atop an ornate base with small, round, molded handles. Commonly found with an enameled exterior and interior. (Czech Republic)

## Unknown Swirl-Style Pans

### Fig 10. Swirl-style pan with scalloped base (I)

**Width:** 9.5 in. / 24 cm
**Height:** 3.7 in. / 9.5 cm
**Weight:** 8.4 lbs. / 3.8 kg
**Volume:** 13 cups
**Value:** $250–$300
**Rarity:** ★★★★★

**Description**
Swirl-style design sitting on a scalloped base, with welded-on handles with an enamel interior. Extremely rare. (Czech Republic)

# Unknown Swirl-Style Pans

## Fig 11. Swirl Style Pan with Scalloped Base II

**Width:** 8.2 in. / 20.8 cm
**Height:** 8.2 in. / 20.8 cm
**Weight:** 5.3 lbs. / 2.4 kg
**Volume:** 8 cups
**Value:** $250–$300
**Rarity:** ★★★★★

**Description**
Rare swirl-style design, sitting on a scalloped base, with welded-on handles. Two are known to exist: one in plain cast iron, and a second with a bluish-gray enamel interior and exterior. (Germany)

# Unknown Swirl-Style Pans

## Fig 12. Swirl Style Pan on a Fancy Base

**Width:** 10.6 in. / 27.1 cm
**Height:** 5.3 in. / 13.5 cm
**Weight:** 6.8 lbs. / 3.1 kg
**Volume:** 15 cups
**Value:** $200–$250
**Rarity:** ★★★★

**Description**

Swirl-style pan on a fancy base with either welded-on or molded handles. Double gate marked on the bottom of the pan. Usually comes with a white-enameled interior and is frequently seen with a blue-enameled exterior. All known examples have originated in the Germany / Czech Republic border region. (Czech/German).

*Inset images courtesy of Marc Wissen*

Unknown Swirl-Style Bundt and Gugelhupf Pans 137

# Unknown Swirl-Style Pans

## Fig 13. Swirl Style Pan with a Solid Tube

**Width:** 8.3 in. / 21.0 cm
**Height:** 3.0 in. / 7.6 cm
**Weight:** 4.1 lbs. / 1.6 kg
**Volume:** 6 cups
**Value:** $200–$250
**Rarity:** ★★★★

**Description**
Swirl-style pan tube with molded handles. Comes with a solid or hollow tube. (Germany)

## Unknown Swirl-Style Pans

### Fig 14. Small Swirl Style Pan

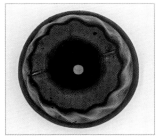   

**Width:** 6.0 in. / 15.3 cm
**Height:** 3.3 in. / 8.4 cm
**Weight:** 1.2 lbs. / 0.88 kg
**Volume:** 4 cups
**Value:** $200–$250
**Rarity:** ★★★★★

**Description**
Small swirl-style Bundt sitting on a plane base with no handles. Extremely rare. (Germany)

Unknown Swirl-Style Bundt and Gugelhupf Pans 139

# Unknown Swirl-Style Pans

## Fig 15. Turks Head Swirl-Style Bundt Pan

**Width:** 10.25 in. / 26.0 cm
**Height:** 3.75 in. / 9.5 cm
**Weight:** 6.4 lbs. / 2.9 kg
**Volume:** 6 cups
**Value:** $250–$300
**Rarity:** ★★★★★

**Description**
Very rare shallow fluted swirl pan. Comes with either gate or sprue marks. Can have a hollow or solid tube. One of only two swirl-style pans known to be produced in the US. (USA)

## Unknown Swirl-Style Pans

### Fig 16. Turks Head Swirl-Style Bundt Pan II

**Width:** 10.25 in. / 26.0 cm
**Height:** 3.75 in. / 9.5 cm
**Weight:** 6.4 lbs. / 2.9 kg
**Volume:** 6 cups
**Value:** $250–$300
**Rarity:** ★★★★★

**Description**
Very rare shallow fluted swirl pan. Comes with either gate or sprue marks. Extremely rare. All known examples from the USA. (USA)
Images

# Unknown Bundt and Gugelhupf Cake Forms

# Unknown Bundt and Gugelhupf Cake Forms

## Fig 1. Octagon—Eight-Sided Bundt Pan

**Width:** 10.25 in. / 26.0 cm
**Height:** 3.75 in. / 9.5 cm
**Weight:** 7.625 lbs. / 3.5 kg
**Volume:** 15 cups
**Value:** $250–$300
**Rarity:** ★★★★★

**Description**
Octagon shaped. Multiple variations exist from different unknown foundries. Extremely rare and very sought after by collectors. (USA)

*Images courtesy of Rhonda Owen*

# Unknown Bundt and Gugelhupf Cake Forms

## Fig 2. The "Oak Leaf"

**Width:** 8.9 in. / 22.68 cm
**Height:** 2.6 in. / 6.70 cm
**Weight:** 8.8 lbs. / 4.0 kg
**Volume:** 12 cups
**Value:** $300–$350
**Rarity:** ★★★★

**Description**
Highly collectible fluted cake form depicting oak leaves. Possibly unmarked Gottbill shallow gugelhupf cake form illustrated in the Gottbill catalog (fig. 20). (Germany)

## Unknown Bundt and Gugelhupf Cake Forms

### Fig 2. The evolution of the "Oak Leaf"

The story of the "Oak Leaf" is an interesting one. The "Oak Leaf" is one of the few gugelhupf pans that have examples that show an evolution of the pan over time. Early versions of the pan had gate marks and either no handles or rounded handles that were welded on. A later version must have been side gated, because it shows no gate marks. It still had the rounded handles, but they were thicker. The last version added fancy, welded-on handles.

Two poor-quality reproductions entered the market. They are easily spotted by the thinner tube, square handles, and poor-quality casting on the bottom of the pan.[50]

With the discovery of the 1933 Gottbill Ironworks catalog, there has been speculation that the "Oak Leaf" was actually the shallow gugelhupf cake form illustrated in the Gottbill catalog (fig. 20). The claim is disputed because the illustration in the catalog differs from the "Oak Leaf" in that it shows a shallow cake form with a tapered tube. The dimensions of the pan listed in the catalog differ slightly from those of the "Oak Leaf." No marked or confirmed examples of the Gottbill shallow cake form are known to exist.

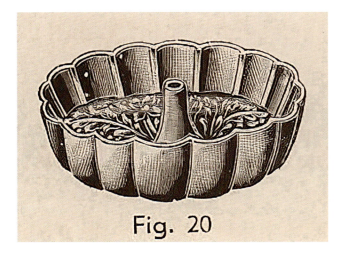

Fig. 20

# Recasts of Nordic Ware Pans

**Nordic Ware**

**Nordic Ware mark visible on recast**

Several cast-iron Bundt pans have recently entered the market in Germany and the Czech Republic that appear to be new recasts of current Nordic Ware aluminum Bundt® pans. Not only are they recasts, but some pans appear to have the Nordic Ware logo still visible on the rim of the pan, confirming that the actual Nordic Ware pans are being used as patterns.

The original Nordic Ware Bundt® pans are the "Bavarian," the "Fleur de Lis," the "Heritage Bundt," and the "Jubilee." These pans are still currently available from Nordic Ware.

**Nordic Ware Aluminum Bundt® Pans**

**Bavarian**  **Fleur de Lis**  **Heritage**  **Jubilee**

**Cast-Iron Nordic Ware Recasts[51]**

**Maiden's War**  **Lord Buba**  **Round-a-Bout**  **Ludwig Jubilee**

## Cast-Iron Recasts of Nordic Ware Pans

## Pan detail

**"Lord Buba"**

**Width:** 9.9 in. / 24.9 cm
**Height:** 4.1. / 10.5 cm
**Weight:** 5.5 lbs. / 2.5 kg
**Volume:** 11 cups
**Value:** $200–$250
**Rarity:** ★★★★

**"Ludwig Jubilee"**

**Width:** 9.9 in. / 24.9 cm
**Height:** 4.1. / 10.5 cm
**Weight:** 8.2 lbs. / 3.7 kg
**Volume:** 9 cups
**Value:** $250–$300
**Rarity:** ★★★

**"Maiden's War"**

**Width:** 9.1 in. / 23.1 cm
**Height:** 3.9 in. / 9.9 cm
**Weight:** Unknown
**Volume:** 10 cups
**Value:** $250–$300
**Rarity:** ★★★★

**"Round-a-Bout"**

**Width:** 9.9 in. / 24.9 cm
**Height:** 4.1 in. / 10.5 cm
**Weight:** Unknown
**Volume:** 10 cups
**Value:** $250–$300
**Rarity:** ★★★

# Cast-Iron Recasts of Nordic Ware Pans

## Handles

After the pans are cast, a unique set of fancy handles are then welded onto each pan (the Nordic Ware pans do not have welded-on handles). The handles are significant because some of the pans cast at the Buzuluk foundry have handles that exactly match the fancy handles on the Nordic Ware recasts. The Nordic Ware recasts are sourced in the Czech Republic, in the same area as the Buzuluk foundry. So while not proof-positive, it is possible that the Nordic Ware recasts are in some way affiliated with the Buzuluk foundry.

"Baby Bundts"

"Baby Bundts," sometimes known as "toy Bundts," were never intended to be real bakeware. They were usually used as toys for children to play with. They are extremely rare and sought after by the collector community. Most originate from Germany and are available in most pan styles.

**"Ludwig Jubilee"**

**Buzuluk "Rhapsody"**
Handles on a Buzuluk a.s. shallow cake form.

# "Baby Bundts"

"Baby Bundts," sometimes known as "toy Bundts," were never intended to be real bakeware. They were usually used as toys for children to play with. They are extremely rare and sought after by the collector community. Most originate from Germany and are available in most pan styles.

**Traditional-Style Baby Bundt**

**Width:** 4.3 in. / 10.8 cm
**Height:** 2.3 in. / 5.7 cm
**Weight:** 8.6 lbs. / 3.9 kg
**Volume:** 1 cup
**Value:** $500–$650
**Rarity:** ★★★★

**Baby Fluted Gugelhupf**

**Width:** 4.3 in. / 10.8 cm
**Height:** 1.5 in. / 3.8 cm
**Weight:** 1.75 oz. / 0.02 kg
**Volume:** ⅔ cup
**Value:** $400–$600
**Rarity:** ★★★★★

**Baby Swirl Style 1**

**Width:** 3.75"
**Height:** 1.5"
**Weight:** 13 oz
**Volume:** 1/2 cup
**Value:** $500–$650
**Rarity:** ★★★★★

**"Innocence" Baby Fluted Style**

**Width:** unknown
**Height:** unknown
**Weight:** unknown
**Volume:** unknown
**Value:** $500–$650
**Rarity:** ★★★★★

# Appendix:
# Research Data

# Appendix: Research Data

## Known European Foundry Marks

| Mark | Foundry |
|---|---|
|  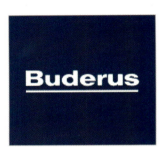 | Boderus Foundry, Hessen, Germany |
|   | "Cousanance," owned by Le Creuset |
|   | Eisenwerk Martinlamitz, Schwarzenbach, Germany |
|   | Eisenwerk Lauchhammer, Lauchhammer, Germany |

Appendix: Research Data **151**

**Mark**

**Foundry**

Frank'sche Eisenwerk, Hesse, Germany

Gottbill sel Erben, Mariahütte, Germany

Olsberg Hütte, Olsberg, Germany

Węgierska Górka Eisenwerk, Węgierska Górka, Poland

Železárny a Smaltovny Bartelmus a.s. Pilsen, Czech Republic. Marked "Pilsen" or "18★70"

# Appendix: Research Data

## Unknown Foundry Marks

| Mark | Description |
|---|---|
|  | The "88" mark can be found on examples of the "Dominion" and on a few "Duchesses." The mark has also been found on a "Monarch," as well as on a traditional-style gugelhupf. All the pans originated in Germany. The "88" mark is frequently accompanied by a separate, single "8" mark. The "88" is believed to be a foundry mark, and the single "8" corresponds to the mold. (Germany) |
|  | Unknown mark found on a traditional-style gugelhupf pan in Germany. The mark possibly belongs to Alfelder Eisenwerk, which was a foundry goods and machinery manufacturer based in Alfeld (Leine), Germany, founded in 1890, which went bankrupt in 1984. |
|  | "C&H" mark with crossed hammers. This mark has been found on a couple of traditional-style gugelhupf pans in Germany. The mark is commonly found on other cast-iron cookware, including German waffle irons and ebelskiver pans. |
|  | The unknown mark "ERM" is located on one of the handles of the "Reichschritter fluted-style gugelhupf pan," reportedly from a foundry in North Rhine–Westphalia. The mark is also commonly found on roasting pans, waffle irons, and cake pans. (Germany) |

# Appendix: Research Data

## Berkley Machine Works & Foundry Company— the "Pilgrim"

The cast-iron "Pilgrim" and the aluminum pattern used to create it were manufactured by Alfred Duncan at the Berkley Machine Works in Norfolk, Virginia, in the early 1970s.

**Cast-Iron "Pilgrim"**  **Aluminum pattern of the "Pilgrim"**

Grind marks on the swirls at 9:00 and 1:00 are clearly visible on the aluminum pattern.

The "Pilgrim" displays the same grind marks on the same swirls at 9:00 and 1:00.

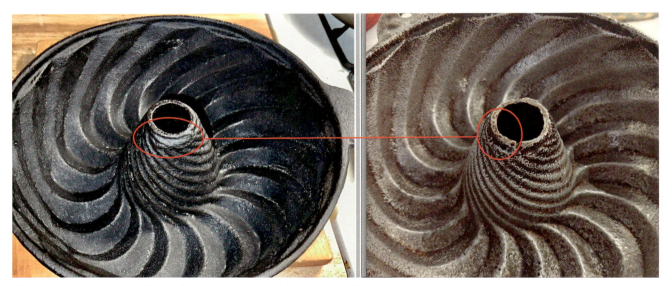

The pattern aluminum displays a flaw at the top lip of the tube, plus a hole in the handle on the left.

The "Pilgrim" displays the same flaw on the lip of the tube, as well as a hole in the handle on the left,

# Appendix: Research Data

### Buzuluk a.s, Muzeum Komárov

Cast-iron cookware display at the Muzeum Komárov, Komárov, Czech Republic[52]

*Courtesy of Muzeum Komárov*

# Appendix: Research Data

## Traditional-Style Gugelhupf Pan Marked "C&H"

Traditional-style gugelhupf pan with molded handles marked with a "C&M" mark with crossed hammers, which is likely the foundry mark. This mark can be found on other cast-iron cookware. The pan also displays "J" and the number "8" marks. Unrestored pan in as-found condition.

*Image courtesy of Jens Duha*

The mark is also found on other cast-iron cookware, including waffle irons and ebelskiver pans found throughout Germany.

*Image courtesy of Jens Duha*

*Images courtesy of Marc Wissen*

# Appendix: Research Data

## Gottbill ser Erben Logos and Marks

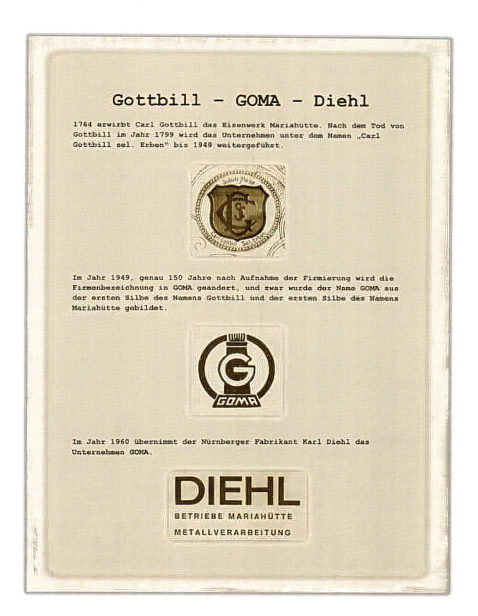

*Image courtesy of Marc Struemper*

# Appendix: Research Data

## Gottbill ser Erben 1933 Product Catalog

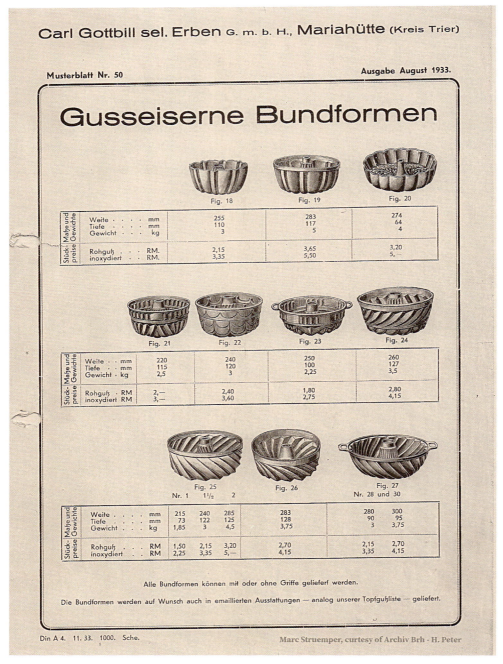

*Image courtesy of Marc Struemper*

# Appendix: Research Data

## Eisenwerk Lauchhammer, Foundry Logos and Foundry Marks

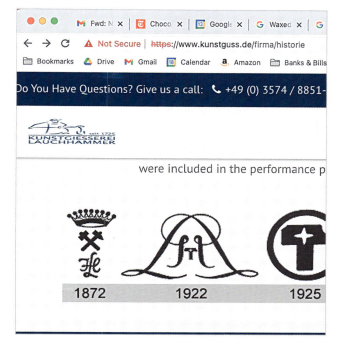

History of foundry marks from Eisenwerk Lauchhammer
*https://www.kunstguss.de/firma/historie*

**Example Marks**

Abb. 248
**Marke, Eisenwerk Lauchhammer**
um die Mitte des 19. Jahrhunderts
Museum Schloss Weißenfels, Inv. Nr. 160/12

Die Marke ist ein erhabenes Kreisfeld, darin befinden sich Hammer und Schlägel und darüber die Grafenkrone der Familie von Einsiedel.
Die Marke befindet sich auf einem Feuerzeug mit einem Soldaten.
Museum Schloss Weisenfels, Inv. Nr. 160/12

# Eisenwerk Lauchhammer, Kunstgussmuseum Lauchhammer

## Visible marks on items in the Kunstgussmuseum Lauchhammer

A Lauchhammer gugelhupf pan on display in the Kunstgussmuseum Lauchhammer

*Photo credit by Bertil Kalex*

Lauchhammer marks found on roasting pans and a "pissoir" (urinal) found at auction in France

# Appendix: Research Data

## Frank'sche Eisenwerk GmbH, Adolfshütte

Undated Frank'sche Eisenwerk product catalog displaying the Frank'sche Eisenwerk foundry mark

# Appendix: Research Data

## The "Reichsritter" Swirl-Style Gugelhupf Pan, Marked "ERM"

Swirl-style fluted gugelhupf sitting on an ornate base with molded handles. Marked with an "ERM" on one handle. (Germany)

Reportedly from a foundry in North Rhine–Westphalia. Up until the 1960s, it produced mainly household goods such as roasting pans, waffle irons, and cake pans.

Other examples of cast-iron cookware with the same mark[53]

# Appendix: Research Data

## History of Węgierska Górka Eisenwerk Foundry Marks

Trademarks of "Węgierska Górka" over the years. *From the left*: the first mark displays part of the Cieszyn Chamber (the crown of the Habsburg coat of arms, the Maltese cross, and the abbreviation TSN for Teschen [German: Cieszyn]). The trademark from the years 1918 to 1936 with the letters "WG" and the trademark used from 1936, with some changes, is used to this day.[54] Some of the first-generation pans display the original "TSN" mark. Some display the word "Teschen." Some pans display both marks.

**1841–1917**  **1918–1936**  **1936–Present**

Example of an enameled oval roaster displaying both the "TSN" and "Teschen" marks

Gottbill sel Erben Gugelhupf Pans

**166** COLLECTIBLE CAST IRON

Known Frank'sche Eisenwerk Gugelhupf Pans

Known Gugelhupf Pans from Eisenwerk Lauchhammer

# Glossary

Bundt pan: A "Bundt" pan is an Americanized version of the European "gugelhupf" cake pan. In southern Germany they were also referred to as *Bundkuchen* (group cake) pans and were served at large gatherings. Northland Aluminum Products, Inc. (later renamed "Nordic Ware, Inc."), an American company, trademarked the word "Bundt" for their version of "bundkuchen pan." So technically (and legally), when someone refers to a "Bundt" pan, they are referring to what is usually an aluminum bundkuchen-style cake pan manufactured by Northland. Because of the Northland trademark, I will use "Bundt" to refer to Northland's pans and will use "Bundt" or "gugelhupf" when referring to all other non-Northland "Bundt" cast-iron fluted cake pans.

custom marks: Some foundries in Europe offered an option to customize a gugelhupf pan with the buyer's initials on it. The two most common pans were the "Twister" swirl-style pan and the traditional-style gugelhupf with "propeller" handles.

enamel: Enamel has been used on cast-iron cookware since the 1920s. While not something seen in collectible Bundt pans in the US, the opposite is true of collectible gugelhupf pans, especially ones from France, eastern regions of Germany, and the Czech Republic. One of the benefits of enameled cast iron is that it does not require seasoning. In the early 1920s, enameling became very popular in gugelhupfs because, especially on the interior of the pan, the enamel provided a superior nonstick cooking surface when compared to a bare cast-iron gugelhupf. In addition, enamel gives a cast-iron pan a more upscale look when compared to that of a bare cast-iron pan. The exterior and interior could be enameled in any color, in stark contrast to the dull-gray look of bare cast iron.

fancy: "Fancy" is a term that is often used to describe an ornate part of a Bundt pan. Bundt pans can have fancy handles, bases, and rims.

foundry marks: Foundry marks are important because they enable collectors to easily identify the foundry where the pan was produced originated. This also makes it easy to determine the age and value of the pan. Marks can come in the form of a foundry name, foundry mark, numbers, or letters, or a combination of these. Marks can have different meanings depending on the foundry.

gate marks: Marks, usually found on the bottom of a cast-iron bundt pan that are the result of a popular method of sand casting. During the casting process, molten iron was poured directly into the mold through thin channels. This enabled distribution of the molten iron into the mold cavity, reducing the number of defective castings. The channels would create "gate marks," which later would be ground smooth but are also still visible as straight lines on the bottom of the pan.

gugelhupf: A "Gugelhupf" pan is the German word for a fluted-style cake pan. In southern Germany, they were also referred to as *Bundkuchen* (group cake) pans and were served at large gatherings. In the Alsace region of eastern France, where gugelhupf pastries are extremely popular, the pans are known as *kouglof*, *kougelhof*, or *kougelhopf* pans. In the Czech Republic, they are known as *babovka* (grandmother) pans.

named pans: While tremendous progress has been made identifying unknown European gugelhupf pans, there remain more than fifty collectible gugelhupfs whose foundries remain unknown. Not knowing the foundry or having any identifying marks on a gugelhupf makes it difficult to identify. For this reason, many of the most popular unknown gugelhupfs now have well-established "names" that have been assigned them by the collector community. So, while in the US a known Bundt pan can be simply referred to as a Griswold "965," a Lodge "L" handle, or a Wagner "A Mold," many of the most popular unknown European gugelhupfs have been given names such as the "Cathedral" and the "Princess," enabling collectors to immediately identify a specific unknown pan. Ideally, these names are a "stopgap" measure that has been put in place until the foundries that produced these unknown pans can be identified.

owner's marks: Quite a few gugelhupf pans contain marks made by their owners. These could be in the form of grind marks in the handles or edges of the pan, numbers or initials scratched on the outside of pans and handles, or even metal tags attached to the handles. In the second half of the nineteenth century, it was not uncommon for there to be communal bakeries in many French and German villages. Villagers would come together to bake bread and cakes in one large communal oven. Sometimes dozens of similar gugelhupfs would be together in an oven at the same time. It is believed that these owner's marks were identifiers that would ensure that everyone would get their own pan back when they were finished baking in the communal oven.

pan styles: There are four main "styles" of cast-iron Bundt or gugelhupf pans: traditional, crown, fluted, and swirl style. The "traditional" style of pan is by far the most common Bundt pan produced in the United States. Crown and swirl styles of pans are commonly found in Germany, France, and the Czech Republic.

rim: Top edge of the Bundt pan.

side-gated pans: Grind marks, usually found on the rim of a cast-iron Bundt pan, that are the result of a popular method of sand casting. During the casting process, molten iron was poured directly into the mold through channels in the side of the mold. These channels enabled distribution of the molten iron into the mold cavity, reducing the number of defective castings. The channels would leave cast marks on the side of the pan. The marks would be ground smooth. This casting method was considered superior to previous casting methods, and casting marks remained on either the top or the bottom of a pan.

sprue marks: Circular marks, usually found on the bottom of a cast-iron Bundt pan, that are the result of a popular method of sand casting. Molten iron was poured directly into the mold through what are known as "sprue holes." After the pan cooled and was removed from the mold, "sprue marks" would be left on the bottom of the pan. These marks would then be ground smooth so the pan would sit (relatively) flat, but the original round sprue marks would still be visible.

tube: Tube rising from the interior of the pan. The tube is what differentiates a Bundt pan from a regular cake pan.

volume: Volume is a way of determining the size of a bundt or gugelhupf pan by measuring how many cups of liquid it can hold. This is typically done counting how many measuring cups of water it takes to fill the pan.

# Bibliography

"About Le Creuset." Le Creuset. https://www.lecreuset.com/about-le-creuset/about-le-creuset.html.

Andrews, Andrew Irving. *Porcelain Enamels: The Preparation, Application, and Properties of Enamels*. Garrard, 1961.

"Blacklock Foundry: A Tale of Fire & Family." *Southern Cast Iron*, June 25, 2019. www.southern-castiron.com/blacklock-foundry-tale-fire-family.

"Bundt Pan Creator H. David Dalquist, 86" (obituary). *Washington Post*, January 6, 2005.

"Costumed Artiste by Jean Agelou, Vintage French Postcard, circa 1910s." Red Poulaine's Musings. https://redpoulaine1.rssing.com/chan-13209931/all_p200.html. Accessed February 17, 2017.

Dept. 113, Frank Aktiengesellschaft, Hessisches Wirtschaftsarchiv. https://www.hessischeswirtschaftsarchiv.de/bestaende/einzeln/0113.php.

"Details zum Wertpapier: Heir finden Sie alle Details zum gewählten Stück." Benecke & Rehse. https://www.aktiensammler.de/br/archiv_branchen_detail.asp?AREA=230&ID=144605.

"Eduard Bartelmus." Wikipedia. https://cs.wikipedia.org/wiki/Eduard_Bartelmus. Retrieved September 25, 2023.

"Eisenwerk Martinlamitz AG" Stock certificate. Benecke & Rehse October 12, 1922

"Enameled Cast Iron." *The Cast Iron Collector* (blog), 2023. https://www.castironcollector.com/enameled.php.

Goldstein, Darra. *The Oxford Companion to Sugar and Sweets*. Oxford University Press. pp. 312–13. Retrieved October 31, 2021.

"The Gottbills." Nunkirchen, 2021. https://www.nunkirchen.de/geschichte/dokumente/die-gottbills/.

Harned, William. "The History of the Griswold Manufacturing Company." Cow Town Collectibles, 1984. http://www.castironcollector.com/griswold.php

"He Saved the Last Czech Enamel Factory." World Today News. https://www.world-today-news.com/he-saved-the-last-czech-enamel-factory-its-not-chinaware-it-lasts-for-generations-he-says. Retrieved June 30, 2022.

"History." Kunstgiesserei Lauchhammer, 2023. https://www.kunstguss.de/en/about-us/history.

"How It's Made: Sand Mold Casting." *The Cast Iron Collector* (blog), 2021. http://www.castironcollector.com/casting.php.

Peter, Claudia, and Harald Peter. *Die Mariahütte—300 Jahre Industriekultur, 1722–2022: Einblicke in die Arbeit unserer Vorfahren; Eine Zeitreise*. Merzig, Germany: Krüger Druck + Verlag GmbH.

Shea, Robert M. "Making Cast Iron Fire Marks." *The Fire Mark Circle of America* (blog), 2021. https://firemarkcircle.org.

"The Story of the True Original." Le Creuse.com, 2021.

"Tunnel of Fudge Cake." General Mills, 2021. https://www.pillsbury.com/recipes/tunnel-of-fudge-cake.

"Wagner Manufacturing Company." *The Cast Iron Collector* (blog), 2023. https://www.castironcollector.com/wagner.php.

Węgierska Górka Eisenwerk. http://turystyka.org.pl/W%C4%99gierska-G%C3%B3rka-historia-m138. Retrieved February 21, 2023.

# Notes

1. "Bundt Pan Creator H. David Dalquist, 86," *Washington Post*, January 6, 2005.

2. Darra Goldstein, *The Oxford Companion to Sugar and Sweets* (Oxford University Press, 2015), 312–13.

3. Marx Rupolt, "Ein new Kochbuch" image, 1581, public domain.

4. Si.edu "Bundt Pan" https://www.si.edu/object/bundt-pan:nmah_1321435 The Smithsonian - National Museum of American History - Creative Commons (CC)

5. "Bundt Pans," MNOpedia, January 6, 2017, https://www.mnopedia.org/thing/Bundt-pan, © Minnesota Historical Society.

6. Nordicware.com, Nordic Ware. 2021, https://www.nordicware.com/heritage.

7. Matt McKinney, "Smithsonian Gobbles Up Bundt Pan," *Minneapolis Star Tribune*, February 24, 2007, retrieved March 1, 2007.

8. "Tunnel of Fudge Cake," Pillsbury.com, https://www.pillsbury.com/recipes/tunnel-of-fudge-cake, ©2021 General Mills.

9. "Lucky Peach's Illustrated History of the Molten Chocolate Cake," *The Inquisitive Eater* (blog), February 12, 2015.

10. "Bundt Pans," MNOpedia, January 6, 2017, https://www.mnopedia.org/thing/Bundt-pan, © Minnesota Historical Society.

11. Nordicware, https://www.nordicware.com/heritage.

12. Si.edu "Bundt Pan" https://www.si.edu/object/bundt-pan:nmah_1321435 The Smithsonian National Museum of American History - Creative Commons (CC)

13. Many thanks to EJ Bogusch for posting many of these tips online for buyers to follow.

14. Photos courtesy of Marc Wissen.

15. Photos of grind marks courtesy of Holger Bogun and Marc Wissen.

16. "How It's Made: Sand Mold," Casting, *The Cast Iron Collector* (blog), copyright 2010–21, http://www.castironcollector.com/casting.php.

17. Robert M. Shea, "Making Cast Iron Fire Marks," The Fire Mark Circle of America, copyright 2005–21, https://firemarkcircle.org.

18. "Eduard Bartelmus," Wikipedia, https://cs.wikipedia.org/wiki/Eduard_Bartelmus, retrieved January 28, 2023.

19. Andrew Irving Andrews, *Porcelain Enamels: The Preparation, Application, and Properties of Enamels* (Garrard, 1961).

20. "Enameled Cast Iron," *The Cast Iron Collector* (blog), www.castironcolltor.com, retrieved Jan 7, 2023.

21. Photos courtesy of Gwen Duncan.

22. "Art Casting," Buzuluk a.s., 2021, www.http://www.buzuluk.com/art-casting.

23. "History," Buzuluk a.s., 2021, http://www.buzuluk.com/buzuluk/history.

24. "He Saved the Last Czech Enamel Factory," World Today News.

25. Český Smalt website, https://www.ceskysmalt.cz/formy-na-peceni, retrieved Jan15, 2023.

26. "Cousances," Wikipedia, https://en.wikipedia.org/wiki/Cousances, retrieved November 19, 2022.

27. "The Story of the True Original," Le Creuse website, 2021, https://www.lecreuset.com/about-le-creuset/about-le-creuset.html

28. "Kunst- und Glockengießerei Lauchhammer," Wikipedia, https://de.wikipedia.org/wiki/Kunst-_und_Glockengie%C3%9Ferei_Lauchhammer, retrieved November 19, 2022

29. Kunstgiesserei Lauchhammer, https://www.kunstguss.de/firma/historie, retrieved November 19, 2022.

30. Die Harzer Eisenhütte unterm Mägdesprung, Ein Beitrag zum Kunstguss im Nordharz by Matthias Reichmann, 214, http://webdoc.sub.gwdg.de/ebook/ga/2002/pub/kunst/01H313/prom.pdf, retrieved November 19, 2022.

31. Photo by Bertil Kalex, http://www.kunstguss museum-lauchhammer.de/, retrieved November 19, 2022.

32. "Martinlamitz," Wikipedia, https://de.wikipedia.org/wiki/Martinlamitz, retrieved March 29, 2023.

33. "Eisenwerk Martinlamitz AG," Benecke & Rehse, https://www.aktiensammler.de/br/archiv_branchen_detail.asp?AREA=230&ID=144605.

34. "Eisenwerk Martinlamitz GmbH," Bloomberg, https://www.bloomberg.com/profile/company/7058837Z:GR#xj4y7vzkg.com.

35. "Industriegeschichte Mittelhessen," Michael Ferger, Marburg, Germany.

36. Dept. 113, Frank Aktiengesellschaft, Hessisches Wirtschaftsarchiv, https://www.hessisches wirtschaftsarchiv.de/bestaende/einzeln/0113.php.

37. "The Gottbills," Nunkirchen, www.nunkirchen.de https://www.nunkirchen.de/geschichte/dokumente/die-gottbills/ Copyright © 2021

38. "Braunshausen (Nonnweiler)," Wimikimedia, https://second.wiki/wiki/braunshausen_nonnweiler Creative Commons. Wikipedia is a registered trademark of the Wikimedia Foundation, Inc.

39. Marc Struemper obtained this information from Harald Peter from the Braunshausen Archiv in Germany.

40. William Harned, "The History of the Griswold Manufacturing Company" (Cow Town Collectibles, 1984), http://www.castironcollector.com/griswold.php.

41. Ibid

42. "Griswold History," Griswold & Cast Iron Cookware Association, www.gcica.org/.

43. David G. Smith and Chuck Wafford, *The Book of Griswold & Wagner* (Schiffler, 2010), 129.

44. "Blacklock Foundry: A Tale of Fire & Family," *Southern Cast Iron*, June 25, 2019, www.southern castiron.com/blacklock-foundry-tale-fire-family

45. "The History of Lodge," Lodge Manufacturing Company, www.lodgecastiron.com/about-lodge/history

46. Ibid.

47. Creative Commons - Wikipedia https://commons.wikimedia.org/wiki/File:Wagner_Manufacturing_plant_in_Sidney_Oh io_1913.jpg

48. http://turystyka.org.pl/W%C4%99gierska-G%C3%B3rka-historia-m138, retrieved 2-21-2023.

49. Red Poulaine's Musings, https://redpoulaine1.rssing.com/chan-13209931/all_p200.html.

50. Photos of the Oak Leaf reproductions courtesy of Marc Wissen.

51. Photos of the "Maiden's War" and the Round-a-Bout, courtesy of EJ Bogusch.

52. Katerina Dobrovolná, Muzeum Komárov, Czech Radio Pilsen, Czech Republic.

53. Photos courtesy of Jens Duha.

54. https://historia.metalpol.com/CIEKAWOSTKI/index.html#115.jpg, retrieved February 21, 2023.

# Index

"88" (mark) 100, 104, 152
965 Fluted Cake Pan (Griswold) 17, 23, 25, 64-66, 89, 185
Adelaide, the ("Triple Crown" series) 25, 114, 121
Aristocracy, the 115
Aristocrat, the 115,116
Baby Bundt, the 148
Baby-style pan 148
Baby gugelhupf pan 148
Baby swirl pan 148
bailed handle 21, 64, 65, 89, 97
Berkley Machine Works 28-29, 153
Big Bake Mold, the 36, 81
bottle opener handles 20, 94
bundkuchen 10, 12
Bundt® 10, 12-13
buying tips 14-15
Buzuluk 30-38
"C & H" (mark)152, 156
Carnival, the 24, 117
Carolina Cooker 14
Cathedral, the 24-25, 118
Cousances 39-40
Crown Jewel series 56
crown-style pans 23, 32-34, 43, 50, 56-60, 74-75, 79, 100-112
custom foundry marks 17
Cyclone, the (unmarked) 24, 124
Cyclone, the (marked Gottbill sel Erben) 24, 62
Cyclone Jr., the 125
Dalquist, Dave 12
Dalquist, Dotty 12
Dolman, the 31, 32, 79, 81
Dominion, the 33, 100, 104, 152
Duchess, the ("Triple Crown" series) 25, 31, 33, 43, 81, 100, 152
Duchess Wolfe, the 44, 61, 126, 129 130
Edeltraud 127
Ein new Kochbuch 11
Eisenwerk Lauchhammer 116, 41-44
Eisenwerk Martinlamitz 45, 46, 150
Ella Helfrich 12, 23
Emperor, the 84
enamel 22
enameled pans 32-34, 36-37, 41-46, 78-81, 100-102, 109, 111-112, 127, 133-136, 163
"ERM" (mark) 120, 152 162

Excelsior, the ("Triple Crown" series) 25, 101
fluted-style pans 24, 40, 55, 65-66, 68, 70-72, 101, 113, 114-121, 139-140, 143
foundry marks 8, 16-17, 150-152
foundry numbers and letters16
"Frank" (marked). *See Frank'sche Eisenwerk*
Frank W Hay & Sons 64, 66
Frank'sche Eisenwerk 16, 47-50, 151, 161
fruit top fluted-style Bundt pan 14, 24, 68
gate marks 19, 20
Gentleman, the 128
Gottbill sel Erben Eisenwerk 8, 16, 51-63, 75-76, 151
Grand Duke, the ("Triple Crown" series) 25, 102
Griswold Manufacturing Company 7, 13-14, 17, 20, 23, 25, 64-66, 69, 73, 89
gugelhupf 7-18, 20, 22-23, 25
handles 18, 20-21, 23
Hoot, the 56, 60
Hubcap, the. See Washington Cake Pan, the
Hurricane, the 24, 126, 129-130
Hurricane, the (marked Gottbill sel Erben) 24, 61, 63, 126, 129-130
J. C. Roberts 20, 67
John Wright Company 14, 24, 68
King, the ("Triple Crown" series) 25, 103
Kingdom, the 85
known foundry marks 7-8, 16, 159, 163
Komárov Ironworks. See Buzuluk
Kouglof 10, 40
Lady, the 31, 34, 81
Lauchhammer Ironworks . *See Eisenwerk Lauchhammer*
Le Creuset . See Cousances
Legacy series (Lodge) 14, 71
Lodge Manufacturing Company 14, 69-71
Lotus Flower, the 31, 35
marked pans 15-18
marks, custom. *See custom foundry marks*
marks, foundry. *See known foundry marks*
marks, gated. *See gate marks*
marks, owner. *See owner's marks*
marks, sprue. *See sprue marks*
marks, unknown *See unknown marks*
Martinlamitz Ironworks. *See Eisenwerk Martinlamitz*
Marx Rupolt 11
Millennial, the 86

173

Monarch, the ("Triple Crown" series) 25, 104
named pans 25
Nordic Ware 10, 13, 14, 145-147
Northland Aluminum Products, Inc. *See Nordic Ware*
Oak Leaf, the 55, 143, 144
Octagon, the 142
oval-shaped Bundt pan, the 87
owner's marks 18
Pauper, the 119
pierced-ear handles 20, 93
Pilgrim, the 24, 28-29, 153
Pillsbury Bake-Off 12
Pillsbury Company 12-13
Poser, the 88
Prince, the ("Triple Crown" series) 25,105
Princess, the ("Triple Crown" series) 23, 25, 106-108
propeller handles 17, 20, 95-96
Queen (unmarked) 110
Queen, the ("Triple Crown" series) 25, 109
Reichsritter, the 120, 162
ring handles 21, 23, 97
Royal King (marked Gottbill sel Erben) 23, 56-57
Royal Prince (marked Gottbill sel Erben) 23, 56, 59, 74-76
Royal Queen (marked Gottbill sel Erben) 23, 50, 56, 58
Rupolt, Marx. *See Marx Rupolt*
Savery and Company Iron Hollow Ware Foundry 14, 24, 72
scalloped (base) 134-135
side gated 67, 76, 144

Small Bake Mold, the 37
sprue marks 19, 20
style, crown. *See crown-style pans*
style, fluted. *See fluted-style pans*
style, swirl. *See swirl-style pans*
style, traditional. *See traditional-style*
swirl-style pans 14, 24, 123-140
"Teschen" (mark). See "TSN" (mark)
traditional-style pan 23, 83-98
"Triple Crown" series 23, 25, 33, 101-106, 109, 114
"TSN" (mark) 78-79, 163
Tunnel of Fudge (cake) 7, 12, 23
Turban, the 31, 38
Turks Head, the 24, 139-140
Twister, the 17, 24, 131-132
unknown marks 14, 25, 152
Vater Brinkhause 14, 133
Wagner "A" mold 14, 23, 25, 59, 74-76
Wagner "B" mold 20, 23, 77, 90-92
Wagner Manufacturing Company 64, 73-77
Washington Cake Pan, the 14, 24, 72
Węgierska Górka Eisenwerk 78-79, 151, 163
Wissen, the 111
Železárny a Smaltovny Bartelmus a.s. 80, 81

## About the Author

### John Briggs, the Cast Iron Chef

Being the Cast Iron Chef enables John to indulge in two of his greatest passions in life: cooking and collecting old cast-iron cookware.

His passion for cooking eventually led him to take a year off from his hi-tech job in Silicon Valley and earn his "Diplôme de Cuisine" through the Le Cordon Bleu program in San Francisco.

Since retiring from hi-tech in 2020, John has launched the popular *Cast Iron Chef* food blog on Facebook. His recipes and cast-iron tips can also be found on his castironchef.com website.

John is also an avid collector of vintage cast-iron cookware. This includes one of the world's largest collections of cast-iron Bundt and German gugelhupf pans.

John is married with five daughters and recently relocated with his wife to Spain, where he continues to collect cast iron and immerse himself in Spanish cuisine, and he is a volunteer chef at José Andrés's World Central Kitchen in Madrid.